THE
Canadian Gardener's Year

THE
Canadian Gardener's Year

A PERPETUAL DIARY
FOR NORTHERN GARDENERS

MARJORIE HARRIS

RANDOM HOUSE
TORONTO

Published in Canada in 1992 by Random House of Canada Limited, Toronto

Canadian Cataloguing in Publication Data

Harris, Marjorie
    The Canadian gardener's year
ISBN 0-394-22256-3

1. Gardening – Canada.   2. Gardening.   I. Title.
SB453.3.C26H36 1992   635'.0971   C92-094640-2

Design: Andrew Smith

Printed and bound in Canada

TABLE OF CONTENTS

ACKNOWLEDGEMENTS

Barbara Schon who helped in so many other ways than editing on this manuscript. Anna Leggatt, Juliet Mannock, Amanda McConnell, hortgurus all.

INTRODUCTION

There was a time when I didn't bother to keep a record of what was happening in my garden. How I regret that now. To be able to look back one or two years has made a significant difference in how I approach the garden.

I now know generally what to expect from the weather and how it will affect my garden. Until I kept a garden diary I didn't realize that May in our area is terrible—wet, usually cold. Its glorious reputation is quite undeserved—at least in Toronto.

The obsessed, who are thinking about their garden through even the cruellest of winters, will find that keeping a garden diary is enormously useful. My diary contains ideas for future borders or beds, wish lists of plants and seeds based on catalogues and books, and all my major redesigning ideas. I know where I will find these fantasies when I need them in the spring. A garden diary, unlike photographs, is meant to be definitive, and looking through it gives an inordinate amount of pleasure.

I leave the diary on a table near the garden, open and ready to fill in the high and low temperatures each day; maybe a comment or two on the weather (humidity, wind, possibility of rain); perhaps some important horticultural event.

Other information entered includes: lists of plants purchased, from whom, and how much they cost (this has become a great way to keep track of how much I spend every year and a good way to compare prices among nurseries). I show where I've put plants and if I've moved them. The following year I'll tick off what survived. Since I move plants around a great deal, I trace their progress through the garden—usually on maps I make of each border. These are regularly updated. When plants are in bloom is tracked from year to year. And I record the ends as well as the beginnings of new life.

I keep all my guarantees from nurseries in the back of the diary. Nurseries will give replacements, but only if you have a corpse and a bill to prove you bought the plant within the past year or two (always check this when you buy a shrub or tree). The bills themselves become a part of the history of the garden.

The garden diary is a record each day of the weather's ups and downs. I've talked to gardeners who've kept them for decades—perhaps some months with little in them other than the temperature. These records have become part of our history.

Memory is faulty at best, and I defy you to remember the exact day the frost moves into, and then out of your garden. But this is critical information. You'll need it to work out when it's safe to put in bedding plants, or to plant seeds. And since the local weather report covers a wide geographic area, you may find that your garden is ahead of or behind the frost dates for your area.

In my garden year book I note my new designs for borders. Below is a sample of one of my designs. It is dated, and given a number. When I change things around I just do a new one. I assign numbers and letters to different parts of the garden. It's my own shorthand for keeping track of things in each section.

SAMPLE BORDER

The border on the opposite page is on a south-facing fence and is about ten feet long and five feet wide (3 m x 1.5 m). I wanted a very soft romantic look because this is close to the deck where we sit every evening in the summer—even when it rains. Scent is important. Sweet-smelling plants are NICOTIANA ALATA, MATTHIOLA BICORNIS (stock), sweet peas and mignonette. For a calming effect I use silvers and greys. Blues

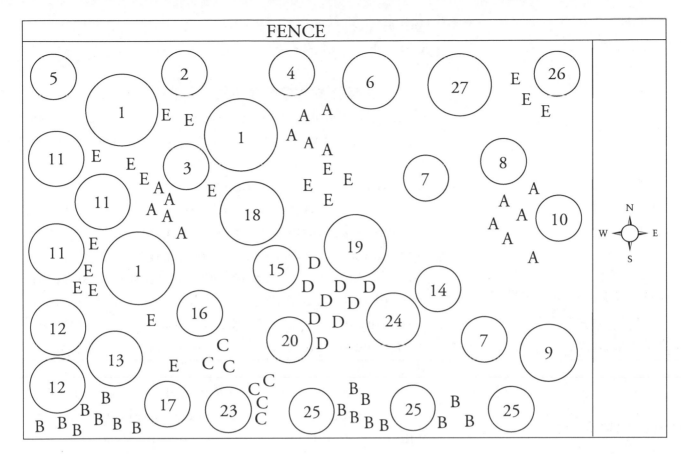

Plant List

1. PAEONIA (peony); 2. CLEMATIS JACKMANII; 3. LYSIMACHIA CLETHROIDES; 4. CLEMATIS MONTANA ALBA; 5. C. COMTESSE DE BOUCHARD; 6. WISTERIA; 7. PEROVSKIA; 8. ASTER 'Harrington's Pink'; 9. ROSA RUBRIFOLIA; 10. ARTEMISIA ARBORESCENS; 11. NICOTIANA; 12. HESPERIS MATRONALIS (white); 13. PHLOX, Mount Fujiyama; 14. IRIS PALLIDA VARIEGATA; 15. VERONICA; 16. SALVIA; 17. PAPAVER (poppy); 18. FILIPENDULA RUBRA; 19. F. 'alba'; 20. GAURA; 21. COREOPSIS VERTICILLATA 'Moonbeam'; 22. LIMONIUM (sea lavender); 23. LAVANDULA (lavender); 24. GLAUCIUM FLAVUM (horned poppy); 25. DIANTHUS 'Mrs. Sinkins'; 26. LATHYRUS; 27. BOLTONIA ASTEROIDES.

Underplanting of Bulbs

A. ALLIUM CHRISTOPHII; B. TULIPA TARDA; C. IXIOLIRION (lily-of-the-Altai); D. NARCISSUS; E. LILIUM.

Notes

and greys are my favourite foliage colours and I put them with other colours to create an aura of softness.

KNOW YOUR MICROCLIMATE

Check a zone map of North America to see which general hardiness zone you live in. Then figure out the microclimate of your garden. This is simple. Record the date of the last frost in your area through the newspaper, then, with judiciously placed thermometers, the last frost date in your garden. When the first frost arrives in your area and when it actually shows itself in your garden may be different dates. You will know because you will see signs of frost on the ground and most of the annuals will look like somebody just stomped on them. Nights will start to get colder and colder and the ground will continue to harden. Record all these events.

In ancient times we were told that if you could sit on the ground naked, it was time to plant. A hand on the ground will do quite nicely. By the time the soil is warm to your hand (mark down this date as well) it will be safe to plant the majority of plants.

Most seeds germinate in the cold and take from eight to fourteen days to do so. Start them at least that many days before the last frost is expected in your area.

SUN MAP

On the previous page make a sun map. Record the dates the sun is at its height in your garden and at what time. You will then know how many hours of sunlight you'll have on that date. Also mark down how far shadows are cast by trees and buildings and how much of your garden is in shadow. This changes constantly as the surrounding trees and shrubs become mature. It's possible to walk by a little tree for two years and not even notice it. Then suddenly you've got a mature plant on your hands. It depends on what you're looking for in the garden at any given moment. We gardeners tend to be very single-minded.

Your own microclimate will reveal far more accurately than any hardiness zone indicator what range of plants you can grow. Microclimates can vary from street to street as well as from region to region. It depends on the height of the land; perhaps you are in a frost hollow at the bottom of a hill. It might mean that you get frost days before your neighbour up the street.

The country is divided into hardiness zones that indicate the general number of frost-free days a year and the annual high and low temperatures. But what they won't tell you is the direction of the prevailing wind. Nor do they take into account the height above sea level. Hardiness zone indication is only meant as a guide to the outside limits of the plants usually grown in your area.

By taking all these elements into consideration you'll be able to figure out what zones you have in your garden. Though this isn't terribly important for the herbaceous plants that retreat underground during the winter, it is crucial for the shrubs and trees you plant.

In your garden you'll probably find that you have more than one zone. Try plants that aren't usually grown in your area or are borderline hardy and see how well they do. You might have a few disappointments along the way, but what is gardening if not perpetual experimentation.

• Put thermometers in those locations that seem to have different conditions. For instance, a solid light fence will hold heat, but an open one will let chilling winds through. Shrubs and trees will act as wind breaks, slowing the fierce winter winds down and protecting plants nearby.

• There are differences in the quality of shade. Temperatures under large canopies of trees will be much lower than in an area where there are stones or there is exposure to the sun for more than six hours a day.

How to Read Plant Symbols

When you buy plants you'll find little symbols that indicate the light requirement for the plants.

○ **Full sun:** needs more than six hours of exposure to the sun every day.

○◑ **Sun/shade:** needs sun for around five or six hours and can tolerate shade the rest of the time.

◑ **Part shade:** will tolerate light shade most of the time; preferably dappled light and a few hours of direct sun.

● **Full shade:** can tolerate areas where the sun doesn't hit directly.

This list also gives you an idea of the different qualities of shade in the garden.

Drainage and Moisture

Find out how well drained your garden is by digging down a foot, pouring in four litres of water and watching how fast it disappears.

• If it just sits there, you are probably on a bed of clay and will have to amend the soil.

• If water disappears in a few minutes, you probably have sandy soil. The drainage is too swift and the soil will have to be amended.

• If it takes about five minutes and goes slowly away, you have very good drainage, and this indicates good soil.

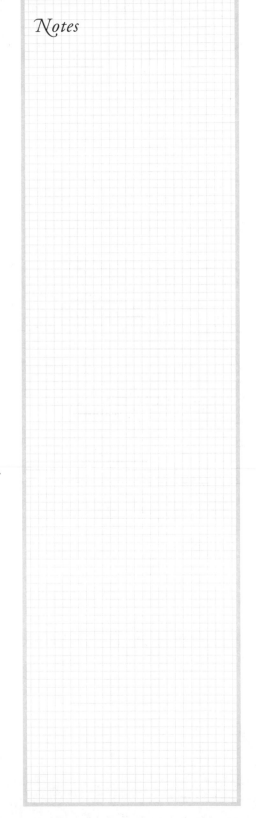

Notes

What almost all plants need more than anything else is good drainage. Few plants thrive with perpetual cold wet feet. Though many will withstand the ravages of drought, most are happiest with good sharp drainage, and it's your job to give it to them and make them as happy as possible.

KNOW YOUR SOIL

To find out more about your soil, take a fistful from a few inches below the surface, wet it, and then give it a good squeeze. Here's what you've got:

loam: will hold its shape initially then crumble;
sandy: falls apart immediately;
clay: just sits there holding its shape.

These are the variations in soil texture. For successful gardening amend the soil if you don't have perfect loam.

Amending the Soil

If there is any problem with your soil and it needs amending the best solution is to add as much compost as you can. Compost is organic matter and the life of the soil depends on it. It will hold moisture and allow nutrients to get to plants more efficiently. Organic matter can be leaf mould (leaves in the process of decaying), well-rotted manure (I prefer sheep to all others); or the very best material of all— compost.

Clay: Add horticultural sand and well-soaked peat moss. Soaking peat moss is incredibly important. Added dry, it will scoop out any moisture there is in the soil in order to create its own bulk. It's always safest to add hot water and let it sit for a week before you use it. Then add as much organic matter as the soil will absorb: compost, sheep manure or leaf mould.

Light loose soil: Add lots and lots of organic matter such as compost, manure and leaf mould.

Moving Plants Around

One of the great joys of gardening is being able to sculpt the shape and thus change the look of your garden. Adding plants is one way, but the best things happen when you start to move things around. You can change your mind constantly and still get something that satisfies you—this may take a long time.

I do exactly what you aren't supposed to do. I move plants in all weathers—rain, heat waves—you name it. But I make sure the plant is going to be as comfortable as possible in the new location.

• Prepare the new site with great care. This is terribly important. Dig in compost or sheep manure below the spot where the roots will sit. This will feed the plants when they need the nutrients and not give them just an instant hit. When you dig up the plant take as much native or local soil with the plant as possible. This will help buffer the shock of transplanting. Water the hole, let it drain, put the plant in the spot and ease in with care. Push plant down with heel of hand but not so hard that you compact the soil. Water almost daily for the next two weeks or until you see new growth appear. Then go back to your usual practice of watering once a week.

It's a good idea to stop moving plants about six weeks before the first frost is due in your garden. But, like many rules in gardening, this is not carved in stone, and you'll get a feel for it. I move plants right up to the middle of October. But I live in Zone 6, and have a very protected garden surrounded by lots of trees. You can usually plant trees and shrubs, and certainly bulbs, long past the time it seems sensible. But give them a chance. Do lots and lots of preparation long before you expect to plant. And then make sure they are well watered. This is especially important for fall-planted trees and shrubs.

You can divide plants in spring or fall—but not during the season in which they bloom. I've done this and they

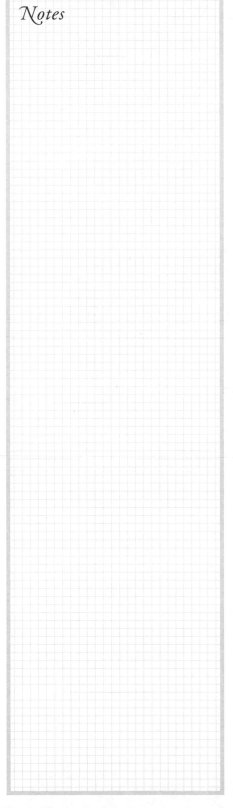

Notes

tend to be extremely grumpy about it. You then have to cut back the blossoms and let the poor things recover from the roots. It will take a year for them to bloom again.

Poisonous Roots and Bulbs
ASCLEPIAS TUBEROSA (butterfly weed); EUPATORIUM RUGO-SUM (white snakeroot); IRIS VERSICOLOR (blue flag); ORNITHOGALUM UMBELLATUM (star-of-Bethlehem); PODOPHYLLUM PELTATUM (mayapple); SANGUINARIA (blood-root).

MOON AND ITS INFLUENCE

I like to look at the phases of the moon and see how they affect the growth of plants and the weather. Ignore this if you want, it's something that amuses me all the time, and amazes me some of the time.

We do know that the moon affects the tides of the seas and now we know it affects the tides in our bodies. So it stands to reason, since plants are made mostly of water, it will affect them too.

I tend to think our ancestors knew a lot more than many of us because they were bound up with natural processes in a way that we've lost.

Here are some interesting things about the moon and the sun:
• The new moon waxes, or increases, until it becomes full. Then it wanes or decreases.
• The sun travels through the entire zodiac, spending one month in each constellation.
• The moon spends three days in each constellation.
• It's said that precipitation falls within three days of the new moon.
• The moon is further from the sun in summer and winter. At its perigee (nearest point) to the earth plants will be vulnerable to pests and fungal diseases.

More tidbits about lunar and solar phases are scattered throughout the book.

Look carefully at what goes on in your garden and follow each variety of plant from year to year. Especially the first plants to bloom in each season—these are your indicator plants. For example, when the snowdrops first flower, this signals the beginning of pre-spring—the date will vary from place to place. This study of climate and the recurrent response of plants to it is called phenology. It is nature's calendar, and this calendar gives us the information we need in order to be the best possible stewards of our land.

In this book there is space for making maps, recording what plants you buy, how they perform, and where you bought them. There are tasks to perform each month. In some cases the information will be repeated because what can be accomplished in one area one month may not be practical until the next in a colder place.

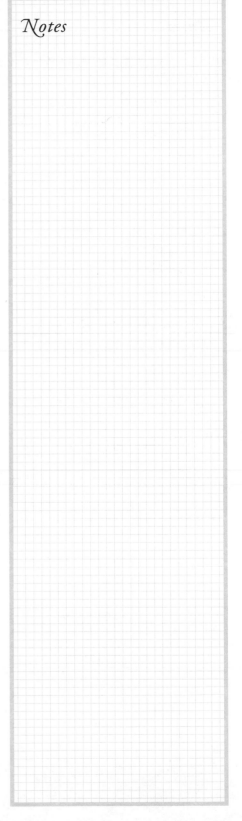

Notes

January

❧

It's catalogue month everywhere. If you feel you are suffering from garden withdrawal, looking through them will banish the gloomiest of moods. But it also means you can put your credit cards into overdrive. Be careful. When you order plants be sure that you have space in your garden for them. When you order seeds make sure that you have room to start them indoors, if they cannot be planted directly into the garden later in the season.

Don't be seduced by gorgeous photographs. Annuals will take a couple of months to get that way. For vegetables—does anything ever look that good? And perennials? it takes them two years to look like anything much at all.

• Make lists before you place your order. Plan where you'll put things by using the map space provided at the end of this month. This will give you a much better idea of what you can actually accommodate.

• If you over-order seeds, keep them in a cool, dry place—preferably in a jar with a bit of baking powder or powdered milk to draw off any moisture. They will probably be able to germinate up to two years from the initial storage time which means you should mark the date on them. I've seen people haul out seeds they've had for years and wonder why they don't have any success with them. They do need a little care. If your expectations aren't high try them before throwing them out. I have hundreds of seeds in my refrigerator at any given time. I never seem to be able to suppress the temptation to collect more.

SEED ORDERS

Ordered from:	Plant:	Germination:	Results:

• Start long-germinating, half-hardy annuals indoors: fibrous-rooted begonias, carnations, gloxinias, lobelias, snapdragons, and sweet peas. Temperatures of 15°C (60°F) are needed for germination.

• To germinate seeds: line a tray with paper, dampen, and sprinkle seeds on it. Cover with clear plastic or a glass lid to keep air humid and give them lots of light.

MAINTENANCE

• Use kitty litter instead of salt on ice patches. It's much safer, more effective, and won't affect lawns or flower borders.

• Make sure ponds with fish don't freeze over. If they do, melt the ice with hot water. Don't break the ice with a hammer—you'll terrify the fish and may deafen them.

TREES, SHRUBS AND FRUITS

• Lichen will grow on apple trees and deciduous azaleas in warm areas with high rainfall. Leave it alone. It's attractive and won't hurt the plants. Spray fruit trees in early January while buds are still in dormancy.

• Lightly thin out spring-flowering shrubs and trees in zones 6 and up.

• If it's warm enough, tend to berry bushes. Raspberries fruit on young wood, so cut out any pale canes that have already borne fruit as close to the ground as possible. Cut back fall-bearing raspberries to ground.

• Gooseberries, and red and white currants fruit on two- to three-year wood. Take the old branches out as close to the soil as possible. Blackberries, loganberries and tayberries fruit on long runners. Get rid of all of them except for six to eight of the longest runners. Tie them to supports. Prune blueberries after six years.

• If it's necessary to spray with a dormant oil spray or to use lime sulphur against the possibility of fungus, do so on a windless, frost-free, dry day. Mulch with compost or manure.

HOUSE PLANTS

• Any house plants that have been in the same pot for more than three years should be repotted. Give all plants a fresh layer of soil and scrub any lime off pots. Check and see if the roots take up more than 50% of the pot space. If they do, choose a new pot that is 3 cm/1¼ in. larger than the current one. Get a good commercial potting soil and moisten with hot water—slit the bag open and fill it with water. Wait until it's been absorbed before using.

• Amaryllis: Once it's finished, cut off the flower head, leave the bare stem, keep in as bright light as possible. Fertilize with 5 mL/1 tsp for each 3 L/1 quart, then cut in half. Use every ten days. In April, reduce water, let leaves die back, and leave it in a sunny spot to go dormant.

GARDEN DESIGN

• Look at your garden. Are you satisfied with the basic structure, the bones of the garden? Is there a pleasing mix of evergreens, brightly coloured stalks of shrubs and trees? Are seed heads left on perennials? Now is the time to figure out what's in the wrong spot and where you'd like it to be next year.

• This is also the time for Creative Staring—working out great fantasies for the future. When designing new borders remember that most plants need a minimum of six hours of sun each day unless they are plants that thrive only in shade.

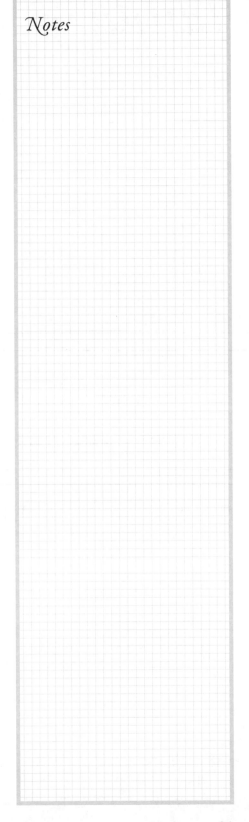

Notes

January

1

2

Here's a handy way to scratch the surface of seeds: line a jar with coarse sandpaper, drop in the seeds, seal and shake. This scoring will help speed up germination.

3

Look for damage in the garden especially after ice storms.
Shake heavy snow from evergreen branches.

4

5

6

January

7

8

9

10

11

Cut back bougainvillaea by two-thirds and feed every 10 days.

12

January

13

*Prune upper limbs and twigs of trees and shrubs
that were root-pruned in autumn.*

14

15

16

17

18

Cut branches of willow, hazelnut or thimbleberry and put them in a vase of water.

January

19

20

House plants love a tepid shower. Set pots in the tub and let a fine or soft spray hit them for at least twenty minutes. This will leach out any salt build-up.

21

22

23

24

Make wish-lists of plants for spring planting.

January

25

26

27

28

29

*Plan to put your patio in a sunny spot;
make a list of all the furnishings that need to be accommodated.*

30

31

February

❧

PLANNING A NEW BORDER

Using the graphed paper of these pages make a drawing more or less to scale—it doesn't have to be accurate, just approximately the same shape.

1. Mark on the graph where plants are now; figure out places where you want to move them.

2. Make a wish-list of plants you'd like to see in place. Mark them on the drawing.

3. Use a code to help yourself. For instance, use numbers to indicate the plants already in place; letters to indicate what you want to put in.

GARDEN DESIGN

The life of a garden is in its constantly changing nature. Keep the good, toss out the merely adequate. This is the perfect time to consult garden and art books for inspiration. Make an overall design, then tackle it section by section each year. By concentrating on only one part you won't get discouraged because you haven't completed the whole thing.

Even if you don't want to tackle it right now, make space for some kind of water element. And think about what you want to do with containers in and around the garden, or on patios and decks.

• Make sure the design fits the style of your house. If possible extend the feeling or soul of your house into the garden. Make it into another room—a garden room.

• Major design elements such as walks, lawns and entertaining areas need careful thought. Good design is never arbitrary. Make an overall scheme that includes all your needs. For instance, if your garden is informal, decks or patios should probably be in a sunny spot, paths should follow the natural inclination of the garden users. If it is more formal move the major elements around on paper to get the most pleasing balance.

• Never try to put too much into the garden at the beginning. It's better to start out with the minimum you need. Add more elements as you become comfortable with them. It is important to have a feeling for what you want from the garden. A serene oasis? An entertainment centre? A children's playpen? A vegetable patch?

• Whatever you put into the garden should have some meaning. Don't clunk in Japanese artifacts willy-nilly if you aren't creating a Japanese garden. Harmonize the various elements in order to keep the integrity of the whole. Imported stones and rocks may take away from rather than enhance the feel of your garden.

• Think of your garden in terms of levels. Start with what trees you have, what trees you want, and then make sure that new trees are in the right place the first time. Shrubs come next. You can probably move large shrubs once if you happen to make a mistake. Small shrubs can be moved with almost the same abandon as perennials—about every three years. Then the perennials—first the large architectural ones, and then on down to the floor of the garden and ground covers.

• In zones 7 and up prune fruit trees. (See January.)

• Check on plants you are overwintering. Add some fresh soil with just a bit of fertilizer and repot if they are getting leggy. Prune back by two-thirds. Get out overwintered fuchsias, geraniums and marguerites. Remove spindly white shoots, prune back to just above the lower dormant buds. Get rid of those that have rotted. Soak any shrivelled corms and plant in a 15 cm/6 in. deep tray of moist peat. As soon as new shoots appear add light. Cut back geraniums (PELARGONIUM ZONALE) and give them a bit of water.

Notes

GARDEN PLAN

February

1

*The first two weeks of February will indicate whether this will be
a wet or dry growing season. If the horns of the moon point down it will be wet;
if the horns point up it will be dry.*

2

3

Choose the right kind of seeds to plant.
Make sure they are drought-resistant if it's going to be dry.

4

5

6

February

7

8

9

*Winter damage to rhododendrons should be
left alone until after the shrubs bloom.*

10

This is the time to start thinking about containers for seeds for an early start next month.
Anything is a candidate—from Styrofoam coffee cups, to egg cartons,
to the bottoms of plastic or paper milk and pop containers.

11

12

February

13

14

For those lucky enough to live in areas with clean snow,
fill buckets with snow, melt, and water new seedlings and house plants.

15

Cut the following branches to make a winter bouquet: forsythia, pussy willows,
wild rose; flowering trees such as apple, cherry, peach and plum. Cut an X
in the base of each cutting and put in water. Change the water every week.
It takes several weeks, but this is a splendid way to have an early spring.

16

17

February

18

19

20

The following plants are wonderful for a February display in warm sunny spots:
ERICA CARNEA *or white* ABELIOPHYLLUM DISTICHUM *(Z6),*
hepaticas, ivy, snowdrops, winter aconites in a small area,
SARCOCOCCA *(Christmas box) (Z8).*

21

For the next three months take cuttings from house plants: leaves, stems, roots or from growth-tips. Cuttings will take about two weeks to form roots.

22

23

February

24

The sight of the beautiful little GALANTHUS NIVALIS *(snowdrop) is a good indicator that you are in the first flush of spring. Make sure to plant them in several places around your garden. Or buy them in pots and put them into the ground later on.*

25

26

27

28

29

If you are in zones 7 and higher, you can probably start turning the soil this month.
Add well-composted manure and don't break up the soil too finely.
Let the weather work for you.

March

DESIGNING THE HERB BORDER

Herb beds used to be called *potagers*—herbs would be combined with salad greens and set out near the kitchen. One of the most charming I've seen was a raised bed with a diamond-shaped design set out in lettuce and the interior filled with parsley, chives, basil and tarragon. Put mint in a pot by itself or you'll end up with a mint garden—it is that invasive.

• Place the herb border near the house in well-drained soil with lots of sun, or on a sunny balcony or patio. Plant your herbs in pots or half-barrels there.

• Strawberry pots are handsome and useful containers for herbs. Make sure that you put some broken clay in the bottom for drainage. Then add soil up to the first hole and put in herbs; keep repeating, planting at the pocketlike openings.

MAINTENANCE

• Clean up roses—remove leaves remaining on plants, rake and remove all old leaves and debris from ground.

• For lime-loving plants—bone meal is a good source of phosphorus and is a slow releaser.

• For acid-loving shrubs—use fertilizers rich in nitrogen such as blood meal.

• Keep an eye out for spring thaws. A freeze-thaw cycle can pitch plants right out of the ground. Add more mulch to keep plants in a temperate atmosphere. Make sure that plants such as rhododendrons are still under wraps.

• When new growth becomes apparent make sure you pull out any weeds, then feed plants with compost and manure.

TREES AND SHRUBS

• Plant evergreens and conifers, grey- and silver-leaved shrubs (artemisia, lavender, rosemary and santolina). Protect delicate shrubs from late frosts.

• Remove stakes from trees after the second winter.

• Tread down frost-lifted trees and shrubs.

• Remove winter protection in two or three stages preferably on an overcast humid day. Cut back protective stalks to ground, clean up dead vegetation and put it, along with any leaves, into the compost.

• In warmer areas, if you decide to move rhododendrons this month, remember that you won't get flower buds for another year. After replanting remove the buds so the roots get all the energy. Keep protected from cold winds for another month. They need at least six hours of sun a day for flower buds to develop and then ripen.

• Ornamental grasses: cut grasses that aren't evergreen back to about 5 cm/2 in. Don't cut back smaller evergreen grasses at all, merely remove dead leaves. With festucas, pull out dead leaves with a good sharp snap.

• Cotoneaster, holly, kalmia, magnolias, pieris and rhododendrons are vulnerable to frost and drying winds when young. As the soil gradually warms up, roots will begin growing. Protect from wind—it might mean keeping on burlap coverings for another month.

INDOOR PLANTS

Start to take cuttings of favourite indoor plants (fuchsias, geraniums) now. This will help the plant bush out and you'll have many new plants. Take a tip 10-12.5 cm/4-5 in. and make a horizontal cut below a leaf joint. Dip in a rooting medium and stick in a fair-sized clay pot. Water in and then put the whole thing into a clear plastic bag. Seal the bag. Keep away from direct light. In two weeks it should have roots. When new shoots appear keep warm, 15-20°C/59-68°F. Water moderately and give the plant lots of light.

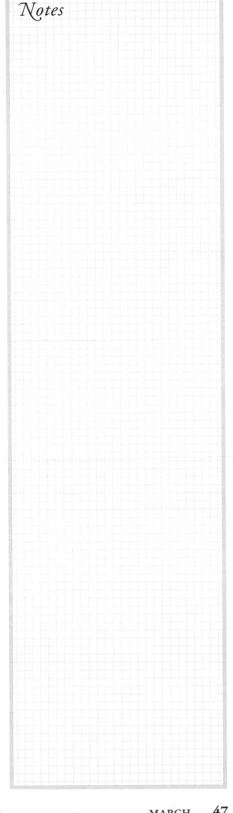

Notes

• When young shoots appear and have grown to 5-7.5 cm/2-3 in., cut off with a clean, very sharp knife below a leaf joint or node. Strip away the lower leaves and dip in rooting hormone. Line up cuttings at the edge of a 14 cm/6 in. pot. Water. Except for geraniums, cover with a plastic bag or glass and keep out of direct light.

PRUNING

There is one rule for all pruning—suit the pruning to the plant. It's picked up with experience.

• Do not prune the following trees now: beech, dogwood, elm or maple. The sap will bleed dangerously. They should be in leaf before you tackle them.

• Do prune: BUDDLEIA, HYDRANGEA PANICULATA, SPIRAEA JAPONICA and TAMARIX. Cut back woody growth made last year. Leave some on new plants.

• After winter-flowering jasmine has bloomed, prune back by half.

• Cut honeysuckle back to one or two stems close to the ground (cut one or two of the main stems back to ground level), remove dead and diseased wood.

• Deciduous shrubs: Prune back to 30 cm/12 in. from soil level.

VINES

Clematis terrifies most people since there is so much confusing information about them. They like alkaline soil so add a bit of horticultural lime to your planting mix.
Try the following:

Group 1

CLEMATIS ALPINA, C. MACROPETALA and C. MONTANA which produce flowers early in the year. Cut back all stems after flowering to 30 cm/12 in. in the first year, to 100 cm/36 in. in the second, and after that just take out weak or dead stems. Or, leave unpruned for several years and just keep them tidy.

• Prune early flowering clematis: C. ALPINA, C. ARMANDII, C. MONTANA, C. MACROPETALA and other hybrids when they're overcrowded, especially C. ARMANDII, C. MONTANA. Cut out old and weak growth, shorten remaining growth by half. New shoots form to carry next year's blooms. C. MONTANA will tolerate some shade. Early clematis like regular pruning and flower on last year's growth—so prune after flowering.
• If mature plants become overcrowded cut back side shoots to a few centimetres/inches of main framework immediately after flowering, leaving one or two buds.

Group 2

These large-flowering hybrids include C. DUCHESS OF EDINBURGH, C. HENRYI, C. LADY NORTHCLIFFE, C. MME LE COULTRE, C. 'NELLY MOSER', C. THE PRESIDENT. They produce blossoms in spring on wood ripened during the previous summer. 'Nelly Moser' produces flowers on short stems commencing in June. In the first year cut this group back after flowering to 30 cm/12 in.; second year cut back to 1 m/1 yd.; thereafter cut back to a strong pair of buds. They often flower again in late summer or fall, so pruning requires thought. Try renewal pruning as soon as flowers fade—cut back ¼ to ⅓ of old shoots to 30-60 cm/12-24 in. of base. Vigorous new shoots will grow to produce an abundant crop of flowers next spring, while unpruned shoots will blossom a second time later this year.
• Large-flowering hybrids blossom in spring and early summer on short side shoots from growth made during the previous year.

Group 3

Hybrids such as C. JACKMANII produce flowers on the current season's stems from July on. First year, cut back to 30 cm/12 in.; second year, reduce all stems to just above the base of the previous season's growth within 75 cm/30 in. of soil level. Annually, hard prune to near ground in pre-spring

Notes

after several years of uninhibited growth; or, for an annual rejuvenation regimen, cut away ¼ to ⅓ of oldest shoots to 30-60 cm/12-24 in. from ground, remove severed shoots, then water and fertilize plants.

• To encourage flowering of wisteria, prune twice a year—pre-spring and mid to late summer. Double pruning will convert new growth into short flowering spurs instead of allowing it to develop into a tangle of leaves and stems.

ROSES

• Pruning roses—take out any winter killed stems; remove crossed branches. With older plants cut out the oldest canes. Prune so that light penetrates the whole shrub, climber or hedge. If you want lower climbers gradually cut back tops.

• When unseasonably warm, tea roses can use drastic pruning. Take back deadwood to base on top-growth buds, and remove weak spindly growth from centre. Reduce all growth by two-thirds making sure all cuts are above an outward-facing bud. The same technique is used for bush roses, polyantha and multiflora roses.

First group: wild species, hybrids, old garden roses and modern shrub roses flower on this year's growth—prune now; or thin and shape by cutting out any shoots that spoil the shape. Remove old or weak canes.

Second group: hybrid tea roses, floribundas and climbers all flower on current season's growth and need annual pruning. Some give huge flowers if cut back to the ground. First year, cut back hybrid teas, floribundas and climbers hard until only two to four buds remain on each shoot to establish a strong root system. Later on, remove weak canes.

• Prune climbing roses: if you want to control their growth, shorten two to five shoots on each side of the main branches to two to three buds of the branch. To prune old roses, remove one or two of the oldest stems down to the base.

• Planting roses: when time draws close to the first day of spring or Easter weekend, plant roses. Start by cutting back any long roots to 20 cm/8 in., and any shoots to three or four strong buds. Remove weak or damaged stems. Soak roots for an hour. Dig hole before removing rose plant from container. Remove all pots including peat and try not to disturb the root ball. It's very important to make sure that the graft is just above the surface of the soil. Fill in with manure or compost.

• Apply fertilizer to roses early enough so spring rains can leach it into the soil well past the roots of plants. This will make food available for new growth when the earth warms up. If you have new trees and shrubs and you've prepared the site well you won't have to do this again for a couple of years.

• Top-dress roses with 5 cm/2 in. of compost or manure.

• Water roses the day before fertilizing.

PERENNIALS

• Perennials that can be moved now: asters, delphiniums, peonies. Keep moving them from now until April.

• Remove leaves from perennials, spread around as mulch. If it's available, get spent mushroom manure (the manure in which mushrooms are grown), and top-dress shrubs and fruit bushes (10 cm/4 in.).

• If winter arrives early and leaves late, plant herbaceous perennials while the soil is heavy, cold and wet. This is especially true for fall bloomers—Japanese anemones, ASTER AMELLUS, A. DUMOSUS, ANTHEMIS, LUPINES, NEPETA, penstemons, scabious, verbascums, ferns.

• Check asters and daisies. If they are bare in the centre of the clump, divide in half. Use as much native (local) soil around the plant when you move it as you can. Replace in the same spot after mixing in a heavy dollop of compost with the soil.

Notes

• HELLEBORUS NIGER (Christmas rose) can be divided once it has stopped blooming.
• Make sure you keep a careful eye on any cloches, greenhouses or cold frames. Temperatures can go over 37°C/100°F if it's a particularly fine day.
• In very cold climate zones, pre-spring planting of all woody plants is the safest method, but don't plant in partly frozen or really muddy soil.
• Check dahlia tubers to see if any sprouting has started. Once shoots reach 6-7.5 cm/2-3 in. long, start taking cuttings for new plants.
• Plant hepaticas, ANEMONE BLANDA, CHIONODOXA; C. LUCILIAE; snowdrops; winter aconite, hellebores around trees and shrubs for protection.

FRUITS, VEGETABLES AND HERBS

• Peas, beans and sweet peas can be planted in zones 7 to 9. Soak peas three to four hours before sowing.
• Gather chicory and dandelion greens.
• Consider intensive sowing if you have a small garden; broadcast seeds in all directions. Weeds will be smothered and you will be discouraged from walking on the bed and compacting the soil. Beds should be 1-1.2 m/3-4 ft. wide. Raise by using soil from the paths around and dig in lots of manure. Sow eggplants, pepper, tomatoes at intervals so you have a succession of seedlings.

STARTING SEEDS UNDER LIGHTS

Start seeds indoors if you have a greenhouse or cold frame. A cold frame is a simple unit without a bottom, with sloping sides, and a window hinged for the top. You can overwinter plants or seeds by adding insulation in the form of hay or straw. You have to watch it though—on a warm pre-spring day the temperature can rise dramatically if you don't prop the top open.

• Before planting indoors check individual seed packages to see what kind of germination is needed, dark or light. Begin with seeds that need the longest germination:

Annuals:

Asters, abutilons, BROWALLIA, cannas (soak seeds in water overnight), impatiens, lobelias, nicotiana, petunias and snapdragons. Half-hardy annuals such as cosmos, African and French marigolds, verbena need to be germinated at 16°C/60°F. Alpines such as campanula and saxifrage take less heat to germinate.

• DIANTHUS; SCHIZANTHUS (butterfly flower); climbers, such as COBAEA SCANDENS (cup-and-saucer vine); ECCREMOCARPUS (glory flower) can all be started now.

• For sowing seeds use 10 cm/4 in. pots, yogurt containers, paper cups, egg cartons, or make your own containers out of newspapers with a little gizmo available from Richter's Seeds. Sow the seeds thinly in sterilized potting soil (or equal parts of soil, peat, sand). Sterilizing soil is not my favourite task. Put soil in a 200°C/425°F oven with a thermometer inserted in the soil. When it hits 90°C/195°F, weed seeds and fungi will be killed off. Spread out to cool and then fill the pot.

• You can start primulas in the greenhouse when temperatures are at 16°C/60°F; outdoor types can be left in the cold frame. Fertilize with superphosphate—15 mL/1 tbsp per 4 L/gallon. Be sure the soil is moist but not muddy. Cover drainage holes in the pot with broken shards of old pots. Mix fine seed with sand. Spread evenly. Cover lightly with soil.

• Put seedlings in as much light as possible. A good combination is artificial cool white and warm white fluorescent tubes 30 cm/12 in. above the seedlings. Nights should be relatively cool 12°C/55°F; and day temperatures 15-17°C/60-65°F.

Notes

LAWNS

If there's water pooling on your lawn it means you have poor drainage. Spike with an aerating tool (don't use a fork—it will compact the soil); remove moss and thatch, top-dress with gravel or sharp sand, if necessary.

• Use a stiff broom to level worm-casts as they appear on the lawn. Fill any hollows created by frost heaving. Add soil a little at a time until it's level.

• This is a good time to trim the edges of lawns and beds.

• Feed lawns with compost or blood meal after a rain when the soil is wet but the grass has had time to dry. Finish preparing areas to be seeded.

• Tons of rain might encourage moss to grow in the garden. My reaction is to pretend that the moss growth was intentional and go look for more. But if this plant bothers you, rake the worst bits off and check out the drainage. It's probably poor and will have to be fixed.

• In zones 7 up, mow the lawn once it begins to look shabby.

WATER GARDEN

• As soon as the ice melts in the pond, clean up and remove any dead or decaying matter. Pull out all weeds and be careful not to trample the edges—the ground will compact like cement. Don't feed fish until temperature is a steady 10°C/50°F, when they are released from dormancy.

BUGS

• On the West Coast and in any wet areas slugs will start their slimy progress through the garden. Start hand picking to get rid of them.

PLANTS IN BLOOM

Shrubs:

ABELIOPHYLLUM DISTICHUM, sometimes called white forsythia (grow in a protected place); CHIMONANTHUS PRAE-COX (Z7); CORYLOPSIS PAUCIFLORA; HAMAMELIS (witch hazel) comes out in spite of icy winds; SARCOCOCCA (Christmas box); STACHYURUS PRAECOX (Z7).

Perennials:

CAMELLIA JAPONICA; CLEMATIS ARMANDII; ERICA CARNEA; flowering cherries and almond; heathers; HELLEBORUS ORI-ENTALIS; MAGNOLIA STELLATA; SCILLA; TULIPA TARDA; VIBUR-NUM X BURKWOODII.

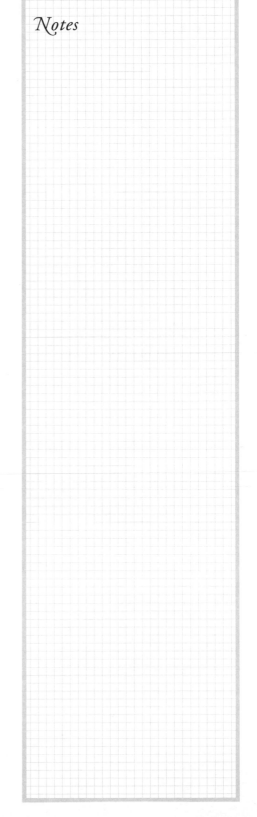

Notes

March

1

2

When the first and second quarters of the moon grow in size put in those plants that produce yield above ground; during the third quarter decreasing phase, plant crops that produce underground. The fourth quarter is good for pulling up weeds and turning the sod.

3

If you plant by the moon, never plant on Sundays
since this day is ruled by the sun and is dry and barren.

4

5

6

Cut back poinsettias by two-thirds to encourage new growth.

March

7

8

9

If you spot crown gall—a sort of disgusting greenish brown mess—
on the roots of roses, you'll have to destroy the whole bush
and leave the spot roseless. Disinfect any tools you used to do this.

10

*Spray fruit trees such as apple, apricot, cherry, nectarine, peach, pear and plum
when the buds burst and just as the bud tips separate into leaves
(never once the bloom has burst open).*

11

12

March

13

Lift and divide perennials once the soil has warmed up.

14

15

As soil thaws and warms up, remove winter protection on a frost-free overcast day.

16

17

18

Newly planted trees may still need protection against drying winds.
Remove protection from others when it seems safe on an overcast, wind-free day.
Keep handy for when frosts are predicted.

March

19

20

Prune late-flowering climbers and shrubs which flower on last year's shoots.

21

This is the month of the spring solstice. Around March 21 is the first day of spring—the vernal equinox. The expanding light and warmth will activate seeds to germinate.

22

23

24

25

Prune roses when the forsythia blooms.

March

26

Mulch and continue to protect delicate shrubs.

27

28

*Don't let warm weather fool you, it's still too early to plant outside.
In some parts of the country plants are coming up; start cleaning up
the garden, pruning where necessary.*

29

*At the end of the month in warm areas, sow hardy vegetables:
broad beans, Jerusalem artichokes, parsnips, peas, salad onions.
Plant when soil is warm and well-drained.*

30

31

April

This is a tricky month. You must be careful of the last frost and the last snowfall even in relatively benign areas such as zone 6. Worry less about the snow than refreezing. A final snowfall isn't going to destroy new plants or seeds. Think of it as very cold rain.

• The sight of ANEMONE NEMOROSA indicates that early spring has arrived. Birches begin to leaf out, and flowering trees such as sour cherry and pear will have white blossoms on them.

• Look for indicator plants that let you know when to start planting. If you live in Saskatchewan, you know it's safe to put in seeds if the poplar bluffs lining the creeks are coming into leaf. Try this method of looking for help from nature itself to make your decisions about when to plant.

• In warm areas plant corn when the apple trees are in bloom, or when the CARYA (hickory) buds are swollen.

PLANTING SEEDS

• If there is still clean snow on the ground melt and bottle it. It's full of minerals and is the best stuff there is for watering seeds for germination.

• Some half-hardy seeds that can be sown outdoors now: CALENDULA (pot marigold); CENTAUREA CYANUS (cornflower); CHRYSANTHEMUM; CLARKIA (godetia); CONVOLVULUS; ECHIUM (viper's bugloss); ESCHSCHOLZIA (California poppy); GYPSOPHILA (baby's-breath); HELIANTHUS (sunflower); IBERIS (candytuft); LAVATERA 'Mont Blanc'; L. 'Silver Cup' (mallows); LOBULARIA MARITIMA (sweet alyssum); NASTURTIUM; NIGELLA (love-in-a-mist); PAPAVER (poppy).

• Cover seeds to a depth four times the length of the seed.

Plant deeper and later in sandy soils. Always plant your seeds more shallowly in clay soils. Firm soil above seed for quicker germination.

• Once the plants have developed two little leaves (these are the cotyledons) they can be moved to individual pots. Make a hole with a dibber or a pencil as deep as the length of the stem; bury right to seed leaves. They will send roots out from the stem and this will keep them from getting leggy. Keep on a window sill, or in a cool greenhouse but shade from direct noonday sun. Scorch and burn is not what a plant needs. Turn once a week so they won't grow in a warped manner, trying to keep their faces in the sun.

• By the first week of May, the seedlings should be 10 cm/4 in. Transfer to a cold frame.

MAINTENANCE

• Restart the compost pile. Turn over the winter detritus and begin to layer once again. Add some manure to speed things up.

• Be sure to treat trellises with wood preservative (non-toxic) before installation and keep them at least a few centimetres/inches above the soil to prevent rotting.

• Keep your eye on the soil near walls and under projecting eaves. These tend to be extremely dry areas. It helps if you dig in lots of organic matter to hold moisture.

TREES AND SHRUBS

Propagation by layering: azaleas, figs, laurels, magnolias, rhododendrons or any shrub with bottom branches low enough to touch the ground and supple enough to bend are candidates. Use a sharp knife and make a nick on the twig where it touches the soil. Replace any heavy soil below the stem with a mix of peat, loam and sand. Peg the nicked section into the soil with wire, bend up stem and support the growing tip above the ground with a can. Cover pegged section with soil. Water regularly. Give a gentle tug to test

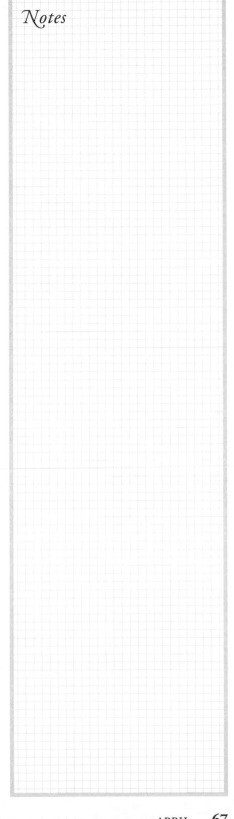

Notes

for new roots. When it resists sever the branch with seca-teurs. Wait a year and then move to its new position.

• The greys will need a light pruning—lavender and san-tolina and other grey dwarf evergreen shrubs.

• Hardy fuchsias coming into bud need to have weak or crowded wood removed and cut back by a third.

• Once spring-flowering shrubs have finished blooming they should be pruned before they start growing. Winter-flow-ering shrubs such as HAMAMELIS, jasmine and viburnum should be pruned now since they bloom on new wood.

• In mild areas, trim back buddleia by about two-thirds; and in cold areas to the ground.

• Prune camellias and magnolias once they've flowered.

ESPALIERING SHRUBS AND CLIMBERS

This is the time of the year to start training shrubs and vines into designs along wires. Make lateral wire supports about 30 cm/12 in. apart. Train branches along the wires and cut out shoots that start growing in between. You can use almost anything to train these shoots along but I find that strong fishing line holds well and is invisible. You have to buy large quantities but it's useful everywhere in the garden. It's a mar-vel to work with and is both weatherproof and flexible.

• Now's the time to fertilize with compost or sheep manure. Leaf mould is excellent as well—it will hold in moisture if you hill up about 15 cm/6 in.

ROSES

Pink buds on roses means it's time to start your spring prun-ing. (See March.)

• Remove suckers from root stocks of roses—these will appear below the bump that indicates the node where the rose was grafted onto parent stock. This is not what you want to happen since the parents, usually ROSA MULTIFLO-RA, are chosen for hardiness, not for beauty.

• Watch for aphids; apply well-rotted manure around the

roses. Leave a ring of bare soil around each, to keep the manure from touching the rose plant. Otherwise, you run the risk of creating rot.

FRUITS AND VEGETABLES

• Gooseberries need rich soil with lots of potash; they can tolerate a bit of light shade. Before planting, remove any buds or suckers on roots; cut back main shoots by half; remove dead, weak or diseased wood. Never plant gooseberries in white pine country. If you find a powdery white growth on gooseberries, cut out infected wood and spray.

• Currants: Plant 5 cm/2 in. deep; cut back to three or four buds above ground. Same as gooseberries.

• Cut out old canes of raspberry bushes, thin new canes and take off about 30 cm/12 in. from the tops.

• Protect peaches and apricots from frost by throwing fine nets on them overnight. Remove during the day so pollinating insects can get at the blossoms.

• Yellow is the colour favoured by most insects. Set up traps of yellow cardboard covered with Tanglefoot—it's sticky stuff. This will attract flying pests.

• Remove the grease-band insect traps applied in fall to fruit trees.

• Check apples for woolly aphid, plums for leaf-curling.

• Transfer tomato seedlings to the greenhouse; plant up in 23 cm/9 in. pots or bottomless pots on pebbles in the north.

• Sow sweet peas with lots and lots of compost. Nip off side tendrils and shoots as they form to concentrate growth on main stem.

• Scilla and grape hyacinths can be left to seed themselves.

PLANTS IN BLOOM

• Alpine pansies; alyssum; ANEMONE (windflowers); AUBRIETA; bergenias; brooms (CYTISUS X KEWENSIS; C. PRAECOX); daffodils; FRITILLARIA IMPERIALIS; F. MELEAGRIS; lily-of-the-valley; MAGNOLIA X SOULANGIANA; MUSCARI ARMENIACUM; PRUNUS JAPONICUS (Japanese cherry); saxifrage; scilla; sweet violets; violets.

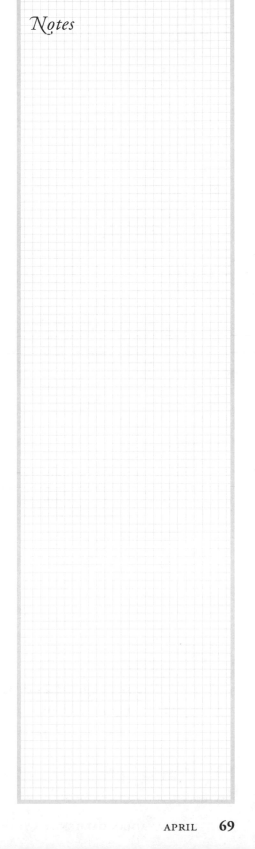

Notes

April

1

2

3

When planting vegetables be sure to intercrop. This means putting slow-growing vegetables next to fast-growing ones, for instance, parsnip and lettuce, asparagus and salad greens. But make sure that short plants near tall ones are shade-tolerant.

Never use insecticides when flowers are open or you'll kill pollinating insects.

4

*Don't seed in the fourth quarter of the moon. The moon affects the germination of seeds by causing them to absorb more water just before it's full.
This is, of course, the time when rains start regularly.
Prune during the decreasing moon when it is in a fruitful sign.*

5

6

April

7

Make sure that trees and shrubs get enough water.
Mulch once the danger of cold weather is over.

8

9

Plant strawberries. Pinch out flower buds for the first season.

10

11

12

*Take photographs of your bulb plantings to help you decide
where you want to move them in the fall, and so that you know
which areas to avoid when you put in new bulbs.*

April

*Plant evergreens and spray the foliage with water regularly
to keep them from getting dried out.*

13

14

15

Mulch fruit with lots of compost, manure or any other organic material,
especially if the weather is dry.

16

17

18

Carpenter's mesh or hardware cloth makes an extremely
effective trellis for climbers—especially sweet peas.

April

19

In zones 7 and warmer, lawns can be sodded or grass seed spread evenly on bare patches. Elsewhere fertilize lawns with compost.

20

21

Forsythia produces flowers on new wood. Once blooms fade, cut to just above ground level.

22

23

24

This is a good time to start preparing the soil for new beds.
By the end of the month, in most zones, you can plant beets,
cabbage, onions and sugar snap peas.

April

25

26

27

Asparagus beds should be cut back and dressed with
hardwood ashes and fertilized with compost.

When the soil starts to warm up, carefully remove winter mulch and throw it into the compost to complete the process of breaking down into organic material.

28

If it's warm enough at the end of the month, thin young fruitlets on espaliered fruit trees over the next several weeks. Remove any tiny pea-sized misshapen ones near the wall. Take one from each pair of buds.

29

30

May

HARDENING OFF PLANTS

• Start repotting dahlias and chrysanthemums into pots larger by one size, cover hole with shards of pots for drainage, then fill with loam or peat-based soil. Place plant in centre and pour soil around the side, tap twice to make it firm; water with tepid water.

• Plant pot-grown alpines now. Make a hole in soil just large enough to take roots, place pea gravel around and under plant—keep weeds down and roots cool in warm weather. Watch first-year alpines for any frost-heaving. Remove dead flower heads but not the foliage.

• Open cold frames so they don't heat up. This is a good place to harden off plants. Cover at night.

SOIL TESTING

Get your soil tested for its pH content. This measures its acidity or alkalinity. Dig down 30 cm/1 ft. in three different parts of the garden, mix together in a half-litre container and take to a garden centre, botanical garden or agricultural station for testing. If soil is too acid, add lime or gypsum to raise the pH level. If soil is too alkaline, add sulphur or aluminum sulphate to lower pH.

PLANT ORDERS

Ordered from:	Date received:	Planted:	Success rate:

NURSERY BOUGHT PLANTS

Purchased from:	*Date purchased:*	*Planted:*	*Success rate:*

BUYING NURSERY STOCK

The Victoria Day weekend is the traditional time to buy bedding out plants from nurseries.

Nursery Tips

• Do not go into a garden centre or nursery without a list. You'll be dazzled by the glorious array of plants set out for your approval. Don't just accept the plants at the front. Pick ones that aren't leggy and have just the slightest bloom showing—this way you'll get good plants and be sure of the colour. Nurseries are famed for mislabelling plants.

• Don't leave your plants in the sun while you are hustling around crazily buying. And never leave them in a closed car.

• As soon as you get your plants home, water them and keep shaded until you can get them into the ground.

• Soak plants for a minimum of five minutes before you put them into well-prepared sites (dig down deep, add compost, water and let drain).

• In zone 3, wait until the wood violets have buds on them before setting out bedding plants.

ANNUALS

Hardy annuals (H)—those that grow well when sown outdoors—can take a bit of frost. Half-hardy (HH) and tender annuals (T) must be started indoors—some, such as lobelia, phlox and salpiglossis, have a short germination period.

• Put out annuals into cold frames for hardening off. Leave the cover open during the day and close it at night. (See April.)

• Plant hardy annuals in window boxes and tubs (wait until all frost danger is over for HH and T annuals). Make sure containers are as large as possible. Use completely new soil in all containers each year. A combination or clay soil prevents shrinkage—it must be heavy enough to make roots secure.

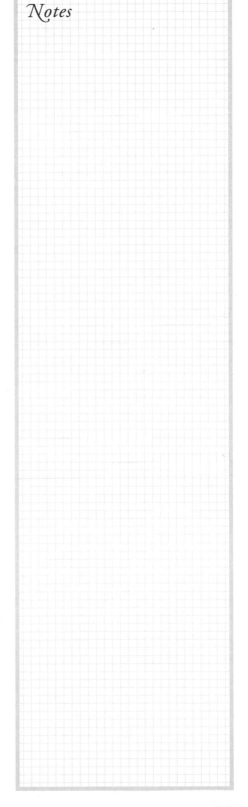

Notes

Mix in a slow-release fertilizer such as compost to feed the plants. Then add a solution of commercial seaweed fertilizer every two weeks.

• Sow the late-summer flowering H and HH annuals in sheltered places under cloches.

• Wait until laburnum and hawthorn trees are in full bloom before putting out HH annuals. Ideal temperatures—10°C/50°F average—15-20°C/59-68°F during the day and 5°C/40°F at night. Transfer annuals to tubs, window boxes.

• Pinch off blooms of annuals to establish strong roots.

• Prick out seedlings.

• When the ladybugs arrive in your garden it's time to set out tomato plants. Plants to attract ladybugs include DAUCUS CAROTA (Queen Anne's lace). If you need more ladybugs, order them. Store in refrigerator until June release time.

TREES AND SHRUBS

• If you must spray for gypsy moth, use Bacillus thuringiensis (it's organic) and do it before the blossoms come out on trees.

• Trim back cedar, cherry laurel and yew drastically. They will look terrible for a while but they'll recover.

• Give all conifers lots of moisture when new growth is expanding, especially young freshly planted trees.

• Plant broad-leaf evergreens such as box, cherry laurel, euonymus, holly, privet, and evergreens such as juniper, red cedar or yews. There will be quick growth on new roots, so water generously. Spray branches continuously since the leaves lose much of their water through transpiration. When planted in slow root growth period, leaves may become dried out in cold dry weather.

• Finish pruning shrubs that flower in late summer or fall on new wood produced this year. Same applies to shrubs with brightly coloured stems planted for winter effect.

• Shrubs with coloured stems to prune now: CORNUS ALBA 'Sibirica'; C. STOLONIFERA 'Flaviramea'; SALIX ALBA; S. A. VITELLINA. These are good ones to consider for winter interest.
• Prune before new growth begins, to keep them eternally young; vigorous new shoots are always longer, more brightly coloured or bloom more freely than older unpruned growths.
• Shrubs to prune now: BUDDLEIA DAVIDII; CARYOPTERIS X CLANDONENSIS; CEANOTHUS; CERATOSTIGMA; ELSHOLTZIA STAUNTONII; HYDRANGEA PANICULATA; LESPEDEZA THUNBERGII; PEROVSKIA; SPIRAEA X BUMALDA; S. JAPONICA 'Anthony Waterer'; S. J. 'Little Princess'; VITEX AGNUS-CASTUS.

VINES

• Prune clematis (check March for which varieties). If you haven't been pruning your clematis vines they'll often have no leaves or flowers in the lower regions. Start the habit now if this has happened.
• Do renewal pruning on CLEMATIS MONTANA and other species which don't need annual cutting back.
• Sow annual climbers. They must have 20°C/68°F to germinate. Sow singly or three to a pot in containers; give as much light as possible.

ROSES

• Fertilize rose plants with generous lashings of compost or a mix of compost and sheep manure.
• Watch roses for aphids, black spot, mildew and rust. Spray with 5 mL/1 tsp baking soda in 500 mL/2 cups of water or insecticidal soap.
• Remove any suckers from roses. Suckers grow from the rootstock which will take over and choke out the grafted rose. Scrape away soil from base—if it is from below the graft it's a sucker. Pull away. Don't cut off at ground level.
• Finish pruning roses before new growth gets too advanced.

Notes

PERENNIALS

• In the first week of May, put flats and pots grown under lights into the cold frame to harden them.

• Plant hardy perennials and alpines grown from seed.

• Don't worry about deadheading chionodoxa, galanthus, leucojum, muscari, scilla. They naturalize by being allowed to set seeds.

• Be sure to deadhead all other big bulbs but don't chop them back. The foliage is vital to make food for next year's blooms. I don't tidy them either. I hate the look of a plant with an elastic band squeezing it around the middle—this will cut off the plant's supply of oxygen.

• You can heel in bulbs while they ripen (leaves will remain green until they have stored up enough food for next year). Dig a trench 15 cm/6 in. deep. Remove flower head, be sure that the fine white roots are not damaged, place in trench, replace soil and firm it but don't crush stems.

• Alternatively, you can store bulbs indoors until fall in a cool dry place. Do this only after foliage has ripened. Clean bulbs by taking off soil and dead skin.

• You can divide GALANTHUS (snowdrops) when in full growth just after they've flowered; divide into single bulbs and replant. Don't let them dry out.

• Tuberous begonias should be potted individually. Delay planting until there is absolutely no danger of frost.

• Twig up plants—use twigs pointing inwards to support plants. Save long elegant twigs for this purpose, they look more aesthetic than huge bamboo canes sticking up all over the garden.

• Stake herbaceous perennials when they hit the half-way mark of their growth. Use only green sticks, ones that are tall but not so tall they stick above the plant—plants that are not staked develop kinks.

• Dividing perennials: try to leave them in place for about three years, but if the centre is bare divide just after flowering.

The plant is at its strongest then, and most likely to withstand the shock.

• Plants to divide now: asters, ferns, goldenrod, ornamental grasses, helenium, monarda, phlox, rudbeckia, perennial sunflowers. Divide when crowns are small enough to survive surgery, so that each section has two or three stems or growth buds. It's wisest to have small vigorous divisions rather than huge ones.

• Cut back hard any alpines that have already flowered; they'll probably re-flower. Divide into several small plants.

• Start biennials from seed for next year: BELLIS PERENNIS (English daisies); CAMPANULA MEDIUM (Canterbury bells); CHEIRANTHUS (wallflower); DIANTHUS BARBATUS (sweet William); HESPERIS MATRONALIS (Dame's rocket); LUNARIA (honesty); MATTHIOLA INCANA (stock); MYOSOTIS (forget-me-not); PAPAVER NUDICAULE (Iceland poppy); PRIMULA X POLYANTHUS; SALVIA HORMINUM.

• Spring mulching should begin this month. I use as much compost as I can, or combine sheep manure, compost and cocoa bean hulls. Do this only when the soil has warmed up, otherwise you'll trap cold beneath the surface. Mulch moderates the soil temperature, keeps weeds down and feeds the plant as it slowly breaks down.

FRUITS AND VEGETABLES

• If there are caterpillars munching away on your fruit trees don't worry—the leaves will come back. Use BT (bacillus thuringiensis) to kill off infections.

• Thin out raspberry canes to six per plant. Get rid of suckers. Keep plants supported with parallel wires if they are in their first season. Thin gooseberries.

• Mulch strawberry plants as soon as fruit appears.

• Ring the bark of any pear or apple trees that won't flower—cut a thin strip 6 mm/¼ in. wide half-way around trunk. Repeat on the other side next year. This reduces the flow of

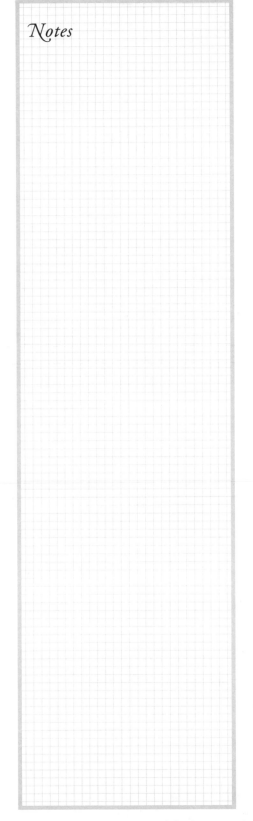

Notes

sap and slows woody and leafy growth. Bind cut with adhesive tape or a lipstick that you've abandoned.

• Thin shoots on espaliered fruit trees and vines and give them a hit of fertilizer—compost and blood meal.

• A continuous sowing of salad crops means a succession of harvests.

• Start fall staples outdoors—brussels sprouts, cabbage, carrots, cauliflower, rutabagas and turnips.

• At the end of month set out eggplants, peppers and tomatoes. Pinch out the growing points of the first two at 15 cm/6 in. for bushy plants.

• Tomato plants should be 15-23 cm/6-9 in. tall with the first flower showing before planting out in a sunny but sheltered spot. Remove any shoots forming where the leaf stalks meet the main stem. Be sure to fertilize with compost.

CONTAINER PLANTING

• Balcony, window box: geraniums (PELARGONIUM ZONALE), fuchsias—repot in fresh potting mix; prune or pinch any that need training to make a good form. Increase watering as growth begins. Make sure they get enough light. Don't set outdoors too early—even though this is such a temptation.

• Harden off geraniums and fuchsias. Put them outdoors during the day and bring in at night if it's still too cool.

• Plant lilies in pots outdoors. Make sure the pots you use for these perennials have a minimum measurement of 35 cm/14 in. Use fresh soil each year. Lilies grown in pots can be moved outside to sunny sheltered spots. Be sure to keep well watered.

• If you want to plant mint but not have it run rampant through the garden try this—cover the bottom of a pot with mesh and plant the mint. Combine two or three types (ginger, apple and spearmint). Then put it in the garden deep enough so the pot isn't obvious. The plant will respond happily to being pot-bound.

• Here are some of the things I love to plant in containers on the deck (usually I work on a colour theme that's soothing because we like to sit on the deck and have our glass of wine and dinner all summer long): CERASTIUM (snow-in-summer) is invasive if left in the garden to ramp about, but perfect in combination with the cobalt blue of LOBELIA 'crystal palace' or one of the trailing kind. Because grey and blue is one of my favourite combinations, I add SALVIA FARINACEA for colour later on and some height, or BROWALLIA which can cope with shade or a combination of sun and shade; ARTEMISIA 'silver queen' is another invasive plant that looks wonderful in large containers. In combination with some summer bulbs such as AGAPANTHUS (lily-of-the-Nile), the effect is glorious in late summer.

• Nerines are spectacular for the fall garden. Exotic and colourful (a glorious pink) they look wonderful massed in pots that you can keep out of the way until they are ready to bloom and need front and centre stage.

LAWNS

• Sow lawn and flower meadow; grass seed germinates well when temperatures don't fall below 8°C/45°F—and all danger of frost is over.

• Fertilize as soon as growth starts. Repair bare patches by scratching up the soil and adding seeds. Top with some compost and water regularly.

• Mowing: As soon as temperatures reach a regular 10°C/50°F, grass starts growing. Never cut more than a third of the height since the green is in the top of the plant. Set the mower at no lower than 5 cm/2 in. up to 7.5 cm/3 in.

Notes

WATER GARDEN

• Start a new water garden: put in full sun if you want to have aquatic plants. This means eight hours of direct sun. Place away from the path of strong winds and from the shade of trees or you'll spend all your time filtering leaves out of it. Put a pond in the lowest part of the garden and make it fit the site. The larger the pool the better your chances of making an ecologically stable area. It should be 60 cm/2 ft. deep. Remember if you have raccoons in your area they will be enjoying the pond as well—probably every night. To discourage them float a ball in the pool.

PLANT LIST

These blue flowers are ones that I enjoy in my own garden. Any cultivar with caerulus in its name is blue. Sometimes I've mentioned cultivars that are especially good but get what you can from your local nursery.

Perennials:
ACONITUM (monkshood); ANEMONE APENNINA; A. BLANDA; A. NEMOROSA; ASTER ALPINUS cultivars; A. X FRIKARTII 'Monch'; AUBRIETA 'Blue Emperor'; BAPTISIA AUSTRALIS; BRUNNERA MACROPHYLLA; CAMPANULA LACTIFLORA 'Prichard's variety'; C. PORTENSCHLAGIANA (dalmation bellflower); CATANANCHE CAERULEA 'Major'; DELPHINIUM; GENTIANA VERNA; GERANIUM 'Johnson's blue' and G. X MAGNIFICUM; HYACINTHOIDES HISPANICUS cultivars; HYACINTHUS ORIENTALIS cultivars; IRIS bearded cultivars; IXIOLIRION; MUSCARI; MYOSOTIS cultivars; NEPETA X FAASSENII (catmint); OMPHALODES VERNA; PULMONARIA SACCHARATA; SALVIA PATENS (gentian sage); SCABIOSA CAUCASICA; SCILLA; TRADESCANTIA; VERONICA AUSTRIACA; V. GENTIANOIDES; V. LONGIFOLIA; V. TEUCRIUM 'Royal Blue'; VINCA MINOR; VIOLA LABRADORICA.

Shrubs:

BUDDLEIA DAVIDII and B. 'Empire Blue'; CARYOPTERIS X CLANDONENSIS (bluebeard); CEANOTHUS (Z8); CERATOSTIGMA PLUMBAGINOIDES (leadwort); PEROVSKIA (Russian sage); SYRINGA X CHINENSIS; S. VULGARIS cultivars.

Annuals:

ANAGALLIS (this is perennial from zone 8 up); BROWALLIA; LOBELIA 'Crystal Palace' or 'Sapphire'; NIGELLA 'Persian jewels'; N. DAMASCENA (love-in-a-mist); SALVIA FARINACEA.

Vines:

CLEMATIS MACROPETALA; WISTERIA SINENSIS.

Notes

May

1

You can start hardy perennials weeks early in most parts of the country.
Even if they get hit by the last snow they will recover.

2

3

Mulch vines thickly at base and make sure they are well watered.
If they're close to a fence or wall, they may not be getting enough water.

4

5

6

Feed shrubs by mulching with compost or sheep manure
as early as possible in the month.

May

7

8

9

Now is the time to plant the less hardy of the conifers:
CHAMAECYPARIS *(false cypress);* CRYPTOMERIA JAPONICA *(Japanese cedar);*
CUNNINGHAMIA *(Chinese fir); hemlocks;* SCIADOPITYS *(Japanese umbrella pine).*

Remove faded flowers from azaleas, camellias, pierises, rhododendrons.

10

*Never plant annuals or any tender vegetables until
you are sure that all danger of frost is over.*

11

12

May

Plant annuals as close as you can to bulbs to cover up the dying foliage.

13

14

15

Plant corn when the apple tree blossoms.

Prune hedges often but lightly to encourage bushy growth.

16

17

Spray a light horticultural oil on shrubs and trees with problems ,
but never when they are in bloom.

18

May

19

20

*Start weeding when plants are young and easy to pull. If you are confused
as to what is actually a weed, go to the nearest field or neglected yard
and identify what's growing there.*

21

Combine rosemary and laurel along with summer bulbs in one pot.
You can bring the whole thing indoors in the winter. Fertilize May through August.

22

23

24

25

Prune honeysuckle, wisteria and other container-grown plants.

May

26

Toward the end of the month start hardening off the plants you've been growing under lights. Use cold frames or a sunny sheltered spot; leave outside during day, bring in during night.

27

28

Put in sunflowers and nasturtiums to attract aphids away from other plants.

29

30

Fertilize spring-flowering bulbs when they start active growth, and again just after the flowers have faded, with a fertilizer rich in potassium. Water it in well.

31

June

MAINTENANCE

• Ladybugs ordered by mail should be released this month. Place them about 7 m/20 ft. apart at the bottom of plants in spots that have been watered and mulched lightly. If you've got lots of larvae and there are bugs for them to feed on they will happily stay. Make sure there is water in the garden for them.

TREES AND SHRUBS

• When pruning make sure all your tools are clean, sharp and well oiled. Sharpen secateurs with fine steel wool.
• Clip off the deadheads of early flowering shrubs such as lilacs and give them a good hit of compost.
• Deadhead rhododendrons and azaleas. Leave faded flowers alone and save some seed of VIBURNUM OPULUS.
• Mulch ornamental shrubs, trees and perennials. I try to mulch as deeply as possible. This preserves water, keeps temperature even.
• Shear evergreens at the edges very lightly to encourage growth inside the plant. If you want to keep a mugho pine small, cut each candle in half.
• To fertilize trees: Ornamental and specimen trees should be fertilized a couple of times a year; at the drip line, insert spade into the ground at an angle toward the trunk. Use liquid fertilizer such as seaweed fertilizer, manure tea or a commercial liquid fertilizer. Apply behind the blade, then firm the soil back in place.

You can also fertilize directly to roots with a special attachment for the hose which will come with instructions for depth and amount of fertilizer. Sink into the ground every 45 cm/18 in. Or make holes 30-45 cm/12-18 in. deep, 5.5-7 m/18-24 ft. apart, insert fertilizer and water the tree thoroughly.

• Look for the delicious purply-black berries on amelanchiers. Common names of this great plant are Juneberries, Saskatoon berries, serviceberries, shadberries or shadblow—depending on your part of the country.

• Deadhead rhododendrons: gather faded flower clusters and snap off before seed pods form. Never use shears; a quick snap off by hand is much safer. Deadhead heaths, heathers, lavenders immediately after flowering. Remove dead flower heads and 20-30 mm/$\frac{3}{4}$ -1$\frac{1}{4}$ in. of the previous year's growth. Follow the natural shape of plant—never cut into old wood.

• Plants to prune in June: deutzia, exochorda and spiraea. Since they all produce new growth from lower parts of the stems—cut out old wood that's already flowered back to the first strong new shoot. On older plants prune about a dozen or so of the oldest stems to ground level. This will keep floppy plants like forsythia and kerria forever new. They'll still flower well and won't lose their natural charm. DEUTZIA, SPIRAEA X ARGUTA (the ubiquitous bridal wreath) will be over by the end of the month. Cut out any old, dead or crowded wood. Remove some of the flowered shoots at ground level to keep them neat.

• Take softwood cuttings from: BERBERIS; CARYOPTERIS; CORYLOPSIS; COTINUS; COTONEASTER; DEUTZIA; EUONYMUS; EXOCHORDA; HIBISCUS; KOLKWITZIA; LABURNUM; LAVANDULA; LESPEDEZA; LIGUSTRUM; LONICERA; POTENTILLA; RIBES; ROSMARINUS; SALIX; SANTOLINA; SYRINGA; VIBURNUM; WEIGELA.

• Prune wall-grown shrubs when they've finished flowering. Cut back CEANOTHUS (spring or early summer flowering) to 5-10 cm/2-4 in.

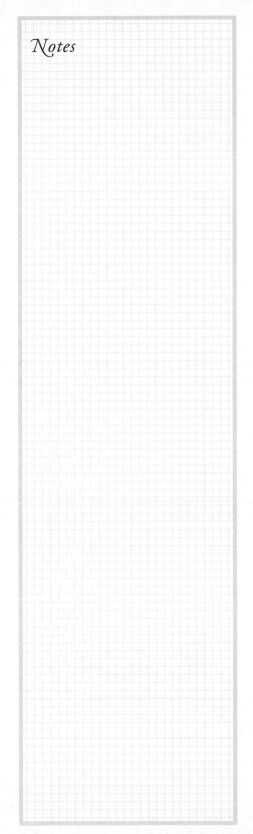

Notes

• To make hydrangeas turn blue add aluminum sulphate to the soil. Then apply a solution of aluminum sulphate—7 g/¼ oz. per 4 L/gallon—weekly from bud break to flowering. Dig in lots of moist peat.

• Trim hedges to keep growth dense right down to the base, and trim flowering shrubs to encourage growth of new shoots to provide next year's flowers. Hand-weed along the bottom of the plantings.

VINES

• Climbers growing on walls may need watering before other plants since soil is often dry if in rain shadow or if wall is high. Water deeply, let dry, loosen surface, then apply thick layer of mulch which keeps down evaporation.

• Prune and tie in new growth. Train new shoots into place and tie when pliable. Cut out weak shoots to prevent overcrowding.

• Sow annual climbers; plant tender or half-hardy annual climbers sown indoors when the mountain ash or hawthorn starts to bloom. Harden off. Add as much compost to your soil as possible.

ROSES

• Fertilize roses just after they've completed one burst of blossom and are about to make new growth for the next. As soon as roses have opened their first flowers, apply a second dose.

• Make sure the soil is moist before applying any dry fertilizer to avoid damaging roots. Therefore, water the day before fertilizing; the next day fertilize—scratch soil and spread rose food. Keep it away from the base of the plant, and concentrate most of it in an area around drip line.

• Watering: water new plants regularly; older plants don't need as much. Water in the morning so foliage is dry by evening and avoid wetting the leaves. Never splash, especially with muddy water. Water deeply enough to soak the soil right down to the root zone. Don't water for several days. Repeat the same operation. Test by checking to see how far the water has penetrated the following day.

• Deadhead roses; cut for vases; never take stems longer than necessary and don't remove more than one or two long ones from any single bush. Cut all faded blossoms off floribundas and HTs as soon as possible so hips won't form. Cut back to a strong, outward facing bud. Continual deadheading removes possible sources of fungal disease. Keep roses deadheaded for a second flowering. But sure to add lots of compost to the roses.

• ROSA RUGOSA cultivars are grown for hips in fall and don't need to be deadheaded.

• Roses, if planted in a container (a window box, for example) will stay small and may not survive a bad winter.

• For bigger rose blooms cut crown bloom off and leave weaker side blooms to flourish. Otherwise just deadhead in the usual way.

• Protect roses against aphids, beetles, black spot and mildew with regular feeding of compost.

• Water containers and hanging boxes every day (twice in really hot weather) and fertilize twice a week.

PLANTS FOR SHADY SPOTS

• Ferns love acid, moist soil in shade. Try some of the following: POLYPODIUM; POLYSTICHUM; clump-forming: ADIANTUM PEDATUM (maidenhair); ATHYRIUM; DRYOPTERIS; POLYSTICHUM; as specimen plants: ATHYRIUM FILIX-FEMINA (lady fern).

• Perennials for the shade: POLYGONATUM (Solomon's seal); PRIMULA; RODGERSIA AESCULIFOLIA; SMILACINA RACEMOSA (false Solomon's seal).

FRUITS, VEGETABLES AND HERBS

• Before you plant strawberries dig in lots of manure or compost to a depth of 30 cm/12 in. in the bed.

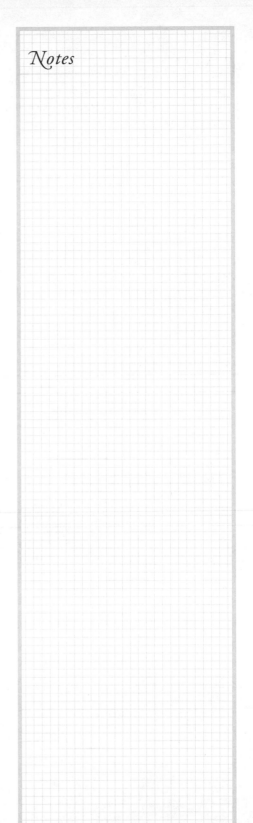

Notes

• Summer prune gooseberries and red currants. Mildew is attracted by tender new growth on tips. This will keep them from becoming infected.

• Drying herbs: tie small-leaved herbs in bundles. Wrap with some porous material to keep dust-free. Hang upside down in a warm, dark dry place. Crush when dry and crisp, then store.

• Basil, chives, mint and tarragon all freeze well—blanch 30 seconds in boiling water, plunge into ice water, drain and freeze. Don't bother to blanch parsley.

• Don't bother transplanting root vegetable thinnings. They probably won't grow properly.

• Transplant brassicas (broccoli, Brussels sprouts, cabbage and kale) but wait until they have four to five leaves before setting out. The most favourable time is in wet weather.

ANNUALS

• Moving containers outside: wait for an overcast day and put in a shady spot, after a few days move to their final location.

• Feed once a week with a diluted fertilizer (I like fish emulsion cut in half of what is recommended in the instructions). Water once or twice a day if necessary.

• When planting seeds, you will need a light covering of soil. Try spreading seeds with a small fine sieve.

• Hand-mist seeds or use an upturned sprinkler head to do the job efficiently.

• Don't drag a hoe through your flower beds. You'll only disturb the root zones. Hand-weeding is one of my favourite chores. Put the weeds into the compost before they develop seed heads—this will cut down on future work.

• Heavy mulching discourages weeds from rooting freely and makes them easy to pull out. You should be weed-free in a couple of seasons.

• Keep bringing out tender bedding plants. Deadhead regularly.

• Keep sowing tender annuals for a steady supply until the snow flies.

• Sowing H and HH annuals in situ means less shock and longer flowering. It will take six weeks for them to reach maturity.

• Annuals in window boxes: renew the soil every year. Mix in a slow release fertilizer before planting.

• Annual climbers: plant outdoors after all danger of frost is over: COBAEA SCANDENS; IPOMOEA TRICOLOR 'Heavenly Blue'; CALONYCTION ALBA (moon vine) grows fast when temperatures at night begin to rise. PHASEOLUS COCCINEUS (scarlet runner bean), HUMULUS JAPONICUS (Japanese hops) will cover anything quickly.

• Water any plants against walls more often than the others. They are probably in a rain shadow.

• Last sowing of annuals: ANCHUSA CAPENSIS (summer forget-me-not); calendula, California poppy, candytuft, CENTAUREA CYANUS (cornflowers); marigold, nasturtium, zinnias.

PERENNIALS

• Sure-fire perennials to grow from seed: aquilegia, pansies, primulas and violas.

• Start hardening off house plants—take them outside into a shady bower during the day, bring back into the house at night as long as it is chilly.

• The smaller the pot, the more watering needed—or plant the pot directly into the soil. There is something called a plunge bed that will also protect house plants and give them a little holiday. Make a wooden frame and fill it with horticultural sand and peat (well moistened). Put the pots in this bed. They won't need as much water.

• Divide perennials after blooming.

• White hollyhocks will attract Japanese beetle, so pick these beetles off in the early morning. They are very destructive.

• Mark what's in bloom in the margins of the book this month to check on the survival rate of your plants from year to year.

• Mulch perennials to keep soil from drying out.

• Cut back delphiniums to 30 cm/12 in. after flowers have

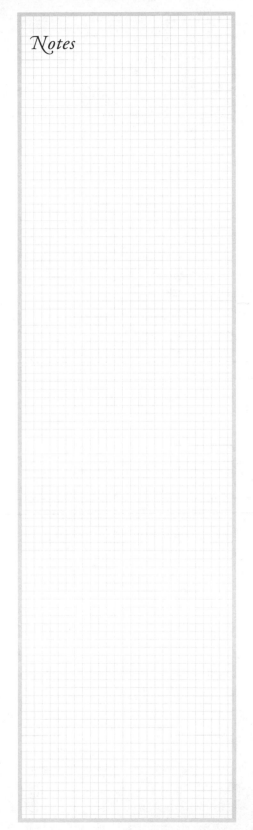

Notes

faded. When new growth starts to show, chop the old stalks to about 10 cm/4 in. from the ground.

• Some other plants that will make a second crop if you cut them back are: CENTAUREA MONTANA; CHRYSANTHEMUM COCCINEUM (painted daisy); ERIGERON (fleabane); lupines; NEPETA. Even if they fail to flower again, the new foliage is much fuller and more beautiful the second time around.

• If you are making a natural garden, leave seed stalks to ripen, seed and naturalize—naturally.

• To make some plants branch out more fully, cut about a third of the stalks back approximately 10 cm/4 in. before buds begin to form. The untouched buds will bloom at the usual time and the others will start a few weeks later. Asters, coreopsis, helenium and PHLOX PANICULATA will all respond to this treatment beautifully.

• Bleeding heart, oriental poppies, Virginia bluebells and any other plants that die down in summer leave vulnerable-looking bare patches. Place markers on the spot so you won't destroy these plants. You can disguise these unsightly empty spots with asters, chrysanthemums, gypsophila, limonium or veronicas which sprawl elegantly.

• Bulbs: finish planting dahlias. Feed every two weeks.

• As soon as the soil is warm enough, plant gladiola corms, unsprouted dahlia tubers. They should be sheltered from prevailing winds in full sun and set into well-cultivated soil.

• Experiment with summer-flowering bulbs such as ACIDANTHERA; AGAPANTHUS (lily-of-the-Nile); GALTONIA; HOMERIA (Cape tulip), HYMENOCALLIS NARCISSIFLORA (Peruvian daffodil); ORNITHOGALUM; SPREKELIA; TIGRIDIA (tiger flower). Try these in pots and directly in the ground to see which gets the best results.

• Divide bearded irises after flowering—lift and cut off outer sections, each with a rhizome attached. Cut foliage into fan shapes, replant each section with rhizome. The rhizome should be showing slightly above the soil.

• Lift and divide PRIMULA (primrose) clumps after flowering; same for POLYANTHUS. Make sure each piece of rhizome has lots of strong roots attached.

CUTTINGS

Cuttings: cut shoots 5-10 cm/2-4 in. below base of a leaf joint, or node. Use a clean, sharp knife or razor blade to make the cut. At the same time, cut back the shoot remaining on the parent plant to next leaf node (otherwise it will rot and look awful). Cut, don't pull, off lower leaves, dip in rooting hormone, make a hole in the planting medium and place the little cutting into it. Make holes with a dibber or a pencil.

• Softwood cuttings: delphiniums, lupines, rosemary, sage, tarragon, thyme and tradescantia, tips of fuchsia, hydrangea, lavender, santolina; the shrubby artemisias: ARTEMISIA ARBORESCENS, A. ABROTANUM, A. ABSINTHIUM, just after first burst of growth.

• Cuttings that like to be in jars of water: African violets, fuchsia, impatiens, tradescantia. After roots appear pot up in peat or loam-based soil mix.

FEEDING AND PROTECTING

• Use fertilizer once a month on all beds until mid-September.

• You don't need to buy expensive compost-starter. Nitrogen is what's needed and you can get that from a hit of blood meal, shellfish wastes (only if you've got something to keep animals out), linseed, soy or cottonseed meal. A layer of fresh grass clippings will heat up a compost faster than anything else.

• If cabbages are bothered by bugs dust them with a mix of salt and flour: 5 mL/1 tsp salt to 1 L/4 cups of flour.

• Spray with tepid water to keep red spider mites away.

• Chances are slugs will be making your life hell by now.

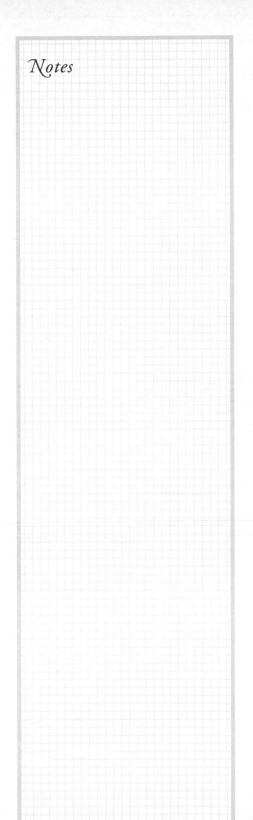

Notes

Get out the slug-stomping slippers and catch them early in the morning. Or, fill a small container with water to which you add brewer's yeast and sugar; don't bother with beer, it's the yeasty brew of life that attracts them. On either Coast, put seaweed (fresh) around beds. It will work until the salt, which they abhor, dissolves. Once rotted, alas, it will attract slugs. But think of this as a trap in which to catch them. Attitude makes a great deal of difference in gardening.

• Spray mildew-ridden plants with 5 mL/1 tsp baking soda to a litre/quart of water. If you add a little soap it will cling to leaves.

• If you have black spot on your roses get the infected leaves out as soon as possible and then use the baking soda spray.

• Manure tea: put sheep manure in a porous bag or a plastic bag with small holes punched all over, and hang it in a large container for a couple of weeks. Cut the tea in half with water and use it to feed plants.

• Juliet Mannock's MPT (manure, peat, topsoil) cocktail: Juliet is one of my garden gurus. She uses this concoction to grow new plants and to start seedlings. It also constitutes at least half of her container mixture each year. Scatter 2.5 cm/1 in. of cocktail over the entire border and water in. Dig in around perennials and shrubs. But not on clematis and delphiniums—omit peat moss and add $\frac{1}{8}$ horticultural lime for these plants.

MPT Cocktail:
$\frac{1}{4}$ composted sheep manure sieved
$\frac{1}{4}$ presoaked peat moss wrung out
$\frac{1}{2}$ weed-free topsoil or good garden loam
Dump ingredients into a garbage can, stir, and mix thoroughly. Use a stick to break up any lumps. Cover, keep moist until put to use. Keep damp but not sodden.

• Never overfeed plants—once a month is usually enough.

• When you water, water deeply but not often.

• Put at least 2.5 cm/1 in. of sheep manure around plants.

BIENNIALS

• Sow biennials in time to make a good start before winter.
• DIGITALIS PURPUREA is a biennial but might stay another year if you cut it back nearly to ground after flowering.
• When lilacs bloom, start sowing biennials such as, BELLIS PERENNIS, stocks, Canterbury bells, forget-me-nots, foxgloves, Iceland poppies and wallflowers.

LAWN

• Grass grows close to the ground where the blades of the lawn mower can't reach it; heavy feeding encourages the growing point of broadleaved weeds to rise above mowing height—they'll get weaker with each mowing.
• Turf grasses are well adjusted to frequent mowing. When you are sowing grass for a new lawn or fixing up bald spots, use a mix of grass seeds. If disease hits one, the others will be able to take up the slack.
• Fescues are more drought-tolerant because the inrolled leaves expose less blade surface to sun and air, which reduces transpiration.
• Making a meadow: take a section of grass and stop fertilizing it, thus starving the soil. Cut mowing back to three times a year. Remove grass clippings. Hold off mowing until the first bloom has finished and don't water native species. They can fend for themselves. Water encourages the less hardy. Eventually fine turf grasses will disappear and be replaced by coarser clump-forming tall grasses and weeds (aka wild flowers) which will infiltrate the bare patches. Only then introduce plant species suitable to your site. Don't bother sowing seeds of a flower meadow until there are open areas between grasses.

WATER GARDEN

Make sure the water garden is aerated. Keep out dead leaves. When filamenous algae appear pull out by hand so they won't envelop underwater plants. Microscopic algae should be left alone—they'll be eaten by other microscopic pond life.

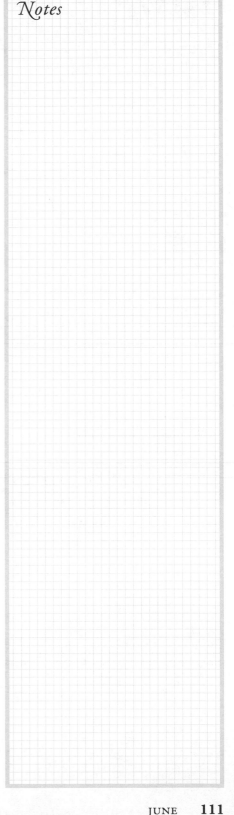

Notes

June

1

2

As indicators of an early summer, the following will be in bloom:
PHILADELPHUS *(mock orange);* ROBINIA PSEUDOACACIA *(black locust);*
SAMBUCUS NIGRA *(European elder); at the end of the season*
early strawberries and cherries will be ripe.

3

Watch when the first quarter of the moon coïncides with the first days under the sign of Cancer. This is the time to put in a special garden with above-the-ground crops. It's also a good time to graft trees.

4

5

6

Plant container-grown trees and shrubs early in the month.

June

In bloom: rhododendrons are in their prime at the beginning of the month;
CORNUS KOUSA CHINENSIS; MAGNOLIA SIEBOLDII;
STYRAX JAPONICUS *(Japanese snowball);* **VIBURNUM PLICATUM** *'Mariesii'.*

7

8

9

Longest days of the year are coming up.

Once the soil warms up, mulch as soon as possible.

10

11

Once the danger of frost is over set out eggplants, peppers, sweet corn,
runner and snap beans, tomatoes.

12

June

13

HT means hybrid tea roses.

14

15

When hawthorn and laburnum are in full bloom, plant pelargoniums (geraniums), fuchsias, begonias, dahlias, cannas, heliotrope and lantanas in window boxes (if done earlier make sure to protect them against night frosts).

Any planting of seeds should be slightly deeper than usual from now on for protection against summer heat.

16

Look around the garden for holes to be filled in with annuals. You can probably buy them on sale by now but they will need a little extra help to do well. Mulch well with compost.

17

18

June

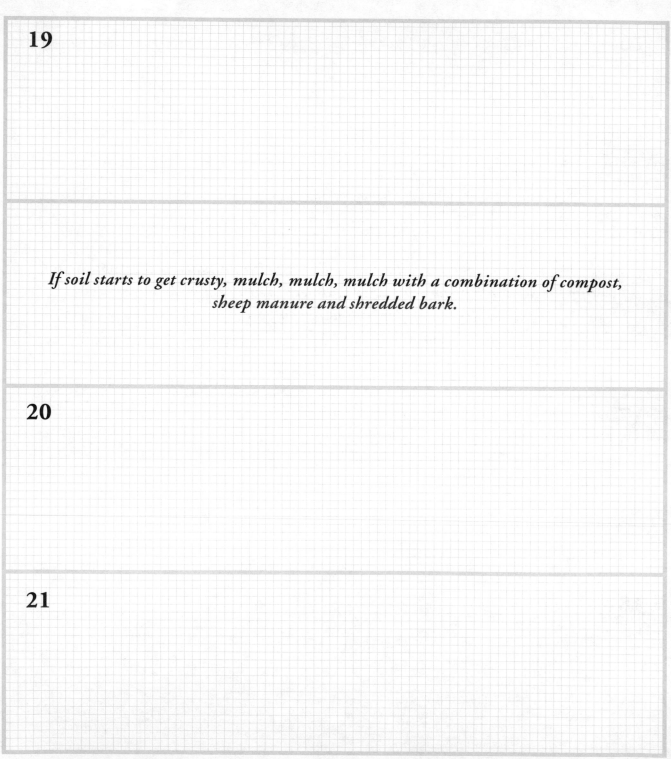

19

If soil starts to get crusty, mulch, mulch, mulch with a combination of compost, sheep manure and shredded bark.

20

21

Remember that crowding plants together will encourage bugs and disease.

22

23

*Leave pyracantha alone because the red berries
are the attraction for winter interest.*

24

June

25

Use rosemary to repel moths.

26

27

A pale lawn means it needs nitrogen. Broadcast blood meal and water it in.

Laburnum pods are poisonous. Leave them alone.

28

*Use pyrethrum to combat chewing insects and rotenone only as a last resort.
These two botanicals will break down quickly which is why
ecological gardeners approve of them.*

29

30

July

You can predict the maturation of plants by the phases of the moon.

New moon, full moon and last quarters are significant in weather prediction. The nearer the moon's change to midnight, the fairer the weather in the following week. The nearer to noon, the fouler the weather.

If the moon changes between:	The weather will be:
10 PM and 2 AM	fair
2 AM to 4 AM	cool, perhaps stormy
4 AM to 8 AM	wet
8 AM to noon	changeable
noon to 2 PM	rainy and blustery
2 PM to 4 PM	mild and showery
4 PM to 8 PM	fair and windy
8 PM to 10 PM	clear and colder

MAINTENANCE

• Keep mowing the lawn regularly but less frequently. If you can't water, set blades higher to avoid sunburnt grass.
• On the patio and balcony water and deadhead. Feed weekly—choose a fertilizer with less nitrogen and more phosphorus and potassium.
• Fertilize tomato plants.

TREES AND SHRUBS

• Continue to take softwood cuttings or semiripe cuttings; semiripe are thicker, have more stored nutrients, and are taken from tips of young shoots. Try BUDDLEIA, daphne, HYPERICUM and lavender. Collect early in the morning and root in a mix of two parts sand (or perlite) to one part peat.

• Hedges such as privet (LIGUSTRUM) need clipping back and TAXUS (yew) should be sheared once over lightly. Cut out reverted branches—this is anything that's green on a yellow shrub or plain on a variegated shrub.

• If a plant turns yellow but the veins stay green you've got a plant with chlorosis. It could mean too much lime for an acid-loving plant. Give a foliar feeding once a week—a spray of chelated iron over and on the leaves.

VINES

• Wisterias should be kept in check. Cut back long twiny side growths to six leaves from main stem. Put coffee grounds around the base to encourage blooming next year.

• Climbers will need extra water, especially young ones.

• Training and tying in new shoots is important; control shoots heading in the wrong direction. This is a creative process because you can seriously affect how vines look.

ROSES

• Deadhead and disbud roses; prune large-flowered, old hybrid teas. Cut back stems without buds by about half their length. Feed. Spray for black spot and mildew with a solution of 60 mL/4 tbsp per L/qt. of Epsom salts and water.

• Give repeat bloomers a moderate dressing of fertilizer. If temperatures drop below 10°C/12°F stop fertilizing at the end of the month.

• Do not use a nitrogen-rich fertilizer which will promote succulent growth—there isn't time for new growth to ripen enough to be able to stand up to frosts. Stop eight to twelve weeks before first frost. For instance, frost hits first in my garden by October 27 or a few weeks later, so I stop by 15-31 August.

Notes

ANNUALS

• Deadhead annuals and prune back lightly after first flush of blossom is past. Fertilize and water well after trimming.
• Replace exhausted plants with new pot-grown annuals, or decorative salad or annual herbs that you've kept in reserve.
• Prick out seedling biennials and repot.

PERENNIALS

• Disbud carnations, chrysanthemums, dahlias—this means pinching out unwanted side buds around central large bud on each stem. Don't do this if you want masses of small flowers.
• In the rockery, anything straggly and brown should have edges cut back.
• Michaelmas daisies may suffer from mildew and fungal rust. Spray at first sign of the fungi.
• Divide spring-flowering herbaceous perennials two weeks after last flowering, when they stop performing. Divide ANTENNARIA; ARABIS; ARMERIA; AUBRIETA; CAMPANULA CARPATICA; CHRYSANTHEMUM COCCINEUM; DORONICUM; HELLEBORUS; PHLOX SUBULATA; PRIMULA; SAXIFRAGA and TROLLIUS. DICENTRA SPECTABILIS and PAPAVER ORIENTALE can be divided and transplanted in midsummer or whenever foliage has started to die back.
• Gladioli, summer-flowering bulbs and corms need top dressing of a fertilizer rich in potassium and phosphorus.
• Bulbs: Most spring flowering bulbs can stay in the same place for years. Daffodils can wait from four to five years or until they become too crowded. Tulips and hyacinths are usually dug up each year once foliage has died back. Muscari and scilla may be divided and replanted at once. Dry off tender bulbs and store.

FRUITS, VEGETABLES AND HERBS

• If you have aphids, try collecting some infected plants and whizzing them up in an old blender. Cut the goop by half with water and strain. Then cut again by half. Spray over the plant. This method seems to work. Try other pests as well. Use slugs to get rid of slugs for example. Adding a little soap will help the spray cling to leaves.

• Watch where butterflies land—they're looking for places to lay their eggs. A cluster of little yellow eggs is a giveaway—pinch them off if you don't want leaf-eating caterpillars nesting in your plants.

• Protect plants from slugs by distributing overturned pots around the garden. Stuff them with scrunched up damp newspapers and collect in the morning when the little devils are looking for a place to sleep. Pop the whole thing into a pail of soapy water to kill them off.

• Layer blackberries, loganberries and blackberry hybrids—bury tips of young shoots 5 cm/2 in. into soil and they'll generate roots from tips.

• Summer prune fruit trees.

• When shallots turn yellow, lift, dry and then store in a cool place.

• Garlic will be blooming. Bend the stalks and let the root bulbs develop. You can use the little bulbils that develop on the bloom heads in salads—mild but delicious.

WATER GARDEN

• Continue to maintain water garden; keep out EQUISETUM (horse tails); GLYCERIA (manna grass); HIPPURIS (mare's tail); TYPHA (cattails).

• Weed bog areas. Keep monkey flower (MIMULUS) or purple loosestrife (LYTHRUM) out. The latter is especially important if you live outside large cities or near water. Even hybrid plants have now been found to produce viable seeds. With great reluctance I've removed all LYTHRUM from my garden. We cannot afford any more damage to fragile wetlands.

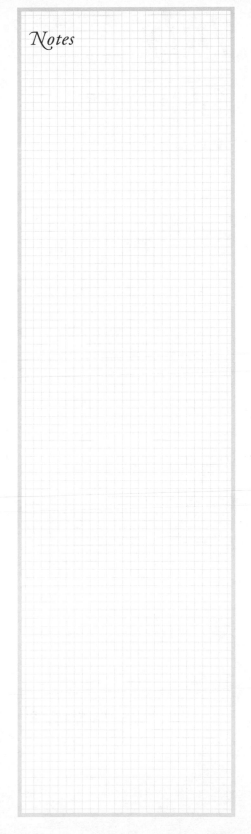

Notes

July

1

2

3

Stop fertilizing woody plants (shrubs and other plants that don't disappear in winter)
after the beginning of the month.

When the moon is new, bugs rest at night and are lively during the day.

4

Some trees will drop leaves during prolonged heat waves—this is a survival strategy. Don't worry about it.

5

6

July

Hold back water from Mediterranean plants; they tolerate drought;
water soft lush plants which will wilt.

7

8

9

10

11

Keep deadheading all plants.

12

July

13

Dahlias are heavy feeders—this means they need lots of fertilizing.
Top-dress every two weeks and mulch.

14

15

16

17

18

Plant fall-flowering CROCUS SATIVUS; C. SPECIOSUS; C. GOULIMYI;
STERNBERGIA LUTEA *and white or pink colchicums.*

July

19

20

Put some blood meal around tomato plants and water in.
Once they take off, stop fertilizing and add compost as a mulch.

21

Cut out all old growth from one-crop raspberries.

22

23

24

25

July

26

Snip runners off strawberries. If plants are past their prime, dig them out and replace with the rooted runners from earlier in summer. This is necessary after two to three years. Leave everbearing strawberries alone to flower.

27

28

29

30

31

Mulch shrubs with compost or sheep manure right now,
for the last big feed of the year.

August

HOW TO COLLECT AND SAVE SEEDS

• Check the garden for plants that are going to seed. It's always enticing to save some seed and see if you can grow the same plants next year. Don't bother with hybrids, they usually don't come true and will revert to the form of the most unprepossessing of their ancestors.

• Collect seed heads when they are dry and brown on a sunny day around noon. Shake them into a brown paper bag, label and keep in a warm dry place until seeds separate. Put the seeds in an envelope, date and seal. Keep in a tightly sealed jar with a bit of powder (baking powder or powdered milk) to draw any moisture. Keep in the refrigerator or any other cool dry place.

• On a still dry day, collect seeds when pods are just about to open. Do this over a period of two weeks in case you happen to miss the best and ripest seeds. Tip larger seeds directly into your hand or a paper bag. If the seeds are small, fix a paper bag over just-ripe seed heads, cut flower stalk and shake head upside down in bag. Make sure the seeds are really dry before storing. If damp, spread on paper on a sunny window sill for a few days. Store in envelopes labelled and dated. Store envelopes in jars with tight-fitting lids. Keep dry at around 5°C/40°F.

• The following hardy annuals can be sown directly into the soil now for next year: BELLIS PERENNIS (English daisy); CALENDULA OFFICINALIS (pot marigold); CENTAUREA CYANUS (cornflower); CHEIRANTHUS (wallflower); ECHIUM PLANTAGINEUM (bugloss); ESCHSCHOLZIA CALIFORNICA (California poppy); IBERIS AMARA (rocket candytuft); I. UMBELLATA (candytuft); LOBULARIA MARITIMA (sweet alyssum); LUPI-NUS (snapdragon); MYOSOTIS (forget-me-not); NIGELLA DAM-ASCENA (love-in-a-mist); PAPAVER RHOEAS (Shirley poppy); SCHIZANTHUS PINNATUS (butterfly flower) and stocks.

TREES AND SHRUBS

This is a splendid time in the garden. CARYOPTERIS (Z6) comes into its own; lavender, PEROVSKIA (Z6), CERATOSTIGMA (Z6) are my favourite blue plants and they are worth the effort to have in the early fall garden.

• Deadhead buddleia and lavender (use flower heads in pot-pourri and to ward off moths in wool).

• Prune now: BUDDLEIA ALTERNIFOLIA; B. GLOBOSA; deutzias; lilacs; PHILADELPHUS (mock orange). Weigelas need prun-ing every two to three years when they become crowded with unproductive shoots at the base, or have weak or dam-aged wood. Do so two to three weeks after flowers fade but not in winter or early spring.

• Take cuttings from semiripe wood: BERBERIS (barberry), box, ceanothus, garrya, lavender.

• Semiripe: wood is considered semiripe as soon as this year's shoots start to get firm at base but are not yet woody. Keep pots outdoors in lightly shaded cold frame and water regu-larly. Plant late next spring.

• Transplant conifers, broadleaved evergreens (nothing ten-der though) when top growth is firm and mature, and the soil is warm enough to make root growth quickly. Give them plenty of water and never let the soil dry out. Be sure to soak them well before planting and continue watering until well established.

• Evergreens can be kept at the same height for years with creative pruning.

• Trim out growing tips of hedges that have gotten too big.

• Prune pines once the candles (new shoots) have matured. Cut back two-thirds or take out the shoot altogether.

Notes

VINES

• Prune wisteria's side shoots to two or three leaves.
• Clematis can be planted now—slant root ball toward the support and dig in 10 cm/4 in. deeper in the ground than in the pot. They are heavy feeders so add plenty of compost.

ROSES

• Deadheading and watering at the base (not on leaves) keeps roses free of mildew and other diseases.
• Don't fertilize roses from now on, especially with any fertilizer high in nitrogen—this encourages new growth which won't ripen enough to withstand winter. However, six weeks before first frost add potassium fertilizer to feed roots. (Phosphate rock, bone meal, cottonseed meal contain phosphorus; seaweed and extracts, manure and compost, granite dust or basalt rock contain potassium.)

ANNUALS

• Nasturtiums bloom from now until the frost kills them off. They won't come true so don't bother collecting seeds. The colour range is fantastic—from a lemony yellow to magnificent reds, and even a palatable orange. They are considered trap plants. Aphids are attracted to them from other plants. Then these pests are easy to get rid of.
• Annuals come into their own. Best to collect—HELIANTHUS ANNUUS (sunflowers); cosmos; LAVATERA 'Mont Blanc' is the best of the lavateras; for scent, plant nicotiana near a patio; SCABIOSA ATROPURPUREA attracts butterflies. ACROCLINIUM, TITHONIA ROTUNDIFOLIA (Mexican sunflowers) and XERANTHEMUM ANNUUM make stunning displays.

PERENNIALS

• Keep fertilizing plants in containers.

• To start rooting cuttings: cut with a sharp knife 15 cm/6 inches below a leaf joint, dip into rooting mix. Make a hole with a dibber in a small pot of sand, vermiculite or other suitable potting mix, and insert the cutting. Water well and cover with glass or plastic and ensure that the cutting remains moist, but does not rot. In a few weeks the cuttings will root and you can transfer them to a 10 cm/4 in. pot.

• Dried flowers should be picked soon: statice, strawflowers and sea lavenders. Collect after they've opened and hang upside down to dry to keep them straight. Store in a cool, dry place wrapped in tissue paper.

• Deadhead regularly, then cut back hard after flowering: centranthus, coreopsis, shasta daisies, gaillardia.

• Plant peonies with no more than 5 cm/2 in. soil over the crown.

• You can divide most plants now, however, leave ferns, ornamental grasses, monarda and scabious alone.

• Cut back biennials after flowering (foxgloves, hollyhocks, Iceland poppies, sweet William). This will produce new growth before winter and blooms the second year. This is also a good time to plant biennials now—the above plus sweet rocket.

• Plant Madonna lilies immediately. Foliage will pop up within a few weeks and remain green.

• Fertilize or foliar feed dahlias, gladiolas, tuberous begonias and tender summer-flowering bulbs.

• Keep deadheading sweet peas.

• Start cutting everlastings: HELICHRYSUM (straw flower); LUNARIA ANNUA (honesty); and MOLUCCELLA LAEVIS (bells-of-Ireland); hydrangeas, ferns, flowers in the daisy family and ornamental grasses. Hang upside down in a dark airy place in small bunches for better circulation.

Notes

FRUITS AND VEGETABLES

• Detach strawberry plants from parents.

• Prune gooseberries and black currants back to one or two of the older fruiting canes and right to the ground; loganberries once finished should be cut back to ground to give this year's canes—next year's fruiting canes—a chance. Remove all but four or five canes.

• Train and prune fruit trees grown against walls. Pears are among the best to espalier—no danger of fruit drop.

• Sow carrots, radishes and turnips for winter supply.

• Put all healthy vegetation left over on the compost. Healthy is the important word. If you suspect anything has a blight or disease get it out of the garden altogether.

• Artichoke looks elegant in the perennial border—it's as decorative as any of the ornamental thistles.

• Asparagus are wonderful to eat but they attract bugs I'd never seen before into the garden—beware the evil asparagus beetle that releases its eggs in a gooey black mass—revolting. Hand-pick and spray with insecticidal soap, then let the late spears turn into ferns. Use rotenone if you get totally fed up with the beetles.

• Garlic chives (ALLIUM TUBEROSUM) are one of my favourite cut flowers. The star-like white umbels last for ages in a vase and weeks in the garden. If you let it go to seed it's prolific; bees are very attracted to this lovely plant.

LAWNS

If drought has hit, be sure to set lawn mower blades higher than normal. Don't worry if your lawn browns up in the heat. It will probably come back quite nicely once you can give it regular watering. A little top feeding of compost will lower stress.

• Leave clippings on grass as mulch.

• Start raising the height of the mower blade and water only if dead dry.

• Cut flower meadow now.

• Start sowing new lawns toward end of the month.

• If you are tired of mowing or your water supply just doesn't warrant a lawn any more, consider installing ground covers. Ground covers are invasive plants. Some varieties are: ajugas; CAMPANULA PORTENSCHLAGIANA; EPIMEDIUM X RUBRUM; HEDERA HELIX (ivy); JUNIPERUS COMMUNIS; J. HORIZONTALIS; LYSIMACHIA NUMMULARIA (thrives in the shade though L. N. 'aurea' is slower to spread but adds lovely golden glow to shady areas); SEDUM SPATHULIFOLIUM; TAXUS BACCATA (yew); THYMUS SERPYLLUM.

Notes

SEEDS

Seeds saved: *Germination:*   *Success rate:*

SEEDS

Seeds saved: *Germination:*   *Success rate:*

August

1

2

3

This is the month when everything becomes torpid including bugs and diseases.
The days are starting to wane and the fruit of the mountain ash is beginning to appear.

It's time to start saving seeds for next year—a fascinating exercise and one worth the small effort required.

4

Don't prune lavender now. Cut away old faded flower spikes for a neat appearance. In very cold areas leave on until spring.

5

6

August

7

8

Trim back cedars or yews to the spot where the green of needles starts.
The interior will have time to harden up before winter.

9

Trim hedges and care for trees and shrubs much the same as last month.

10

11

12

13

August

14

Take root cuttings from nonflowering shoots of CALLUNA *and* ERICA.

15

16

Prepare bare spots for sowing next month by weeding,
breaking up clods and getting rid of debris.

17

18

19

Unlike climbing roses, ramblers only flower once a year in early summer.
Remove older canes to make room for new. Let go for a couple of years.
Dig in lots of compost and water well.

August

20

21

22

Start dividing plants so they have enough time to take hold before the first frost sets in. End this chore about six weeks before the first frost date. Bulbs, irises and most herbaceous plants can be divided right up to frost.

Collect petals for potpourri—roses, lavender, orange blossoms
and those from any other plant with a lovely scent.

23

This is the season for basil in all sorts of colours. Basil 'Dark Opal' combined with
sedum 'Autumn Joy' and borage, which flops about and self-seeds at will,
is a glorious combination.

24

25

August

26

27

28

Plant bulbs as soon as they arrive: ERYTHRONIUM *(dog's-tooth violets);*
FRITILLARIA IMPERIALIS *(crown-imperial);* GALANTHUS *(snowdrops);*
LEUCOJUM *(snowflakes);* and MUSCARI *(grape hyacinths).*

Continue to plant herbaceous perennials.

29

Pick up all rotting fruit from trees—apples, apricots, cherries, peaches, pears, plums and dump in the compost.

30

31

September

❧

This is the most stable period of weather with long nights and calm skies. Temperatures start to fall; however, there's always Indian summer to look forward to. Any cool clear night with no wind may indicate that a frost is coming.

SEEDS

• Sow the seeds of hardy biennials in situ: CHEIRANTHUS (wallflowers), daisies, DIGITALIS (foxgloves), ERYSIMUM (alpine wallflowers), hollyhocks, LUNARIA (honesty), MYOSOTIS (forget-me-not), ONOPORDUM (Scotch thistle), PAPAVER NUDICAULE (Iceland poppies), VIOLA X WITTROCKIANA (pansies).
• Sow godetia, larkspur (DELPHINIUM).
• Save seeds from poppies, California poppies and marigolds.
• Thin any seedlings planted last month and move to larger pots.
• Cut layered carnations from parent plant.

TREES AND SHRUBS

• Plant evergreens. If it turns windy, protect them from drying out.
• Transplant evergreens now.
• Deadhead flowering shrubs and water if dry.
• Heel cutting: pull shoot away from parent plant, leaving a thin sliver of bark and wood from old stem.
• To prepare newly planted trees and shrubs, remove perennial weeds, keep soil surface loose, water and mulch if necessary. Be careful to avoid damaging roots. Complete hoeing, digging, mulching before leaves drop off but allow them to stay on the ground for extra protection.

• Fall-flowering shrubs: ELSHOLTZIA (Z4) (mint bush) and LESPEDEZA THUNBERGII (pea family) (Z5)—cut to ground in late winter; they bloom on this year's wood.

ROSES

• Stop deadheading perpetual flowering shrub roses and climbing roses. This will give the plants time to harden any new growth.

• Disbud—keep the side buds pinched out.

• By cultivating roses you avoid infection. Remove any leaves infected by black spot or mildew.

• Newly planted hybrid and floribunda roses need hard pruning the first year. Do this when the bush is first planted or when the plant is dormant. Prune stems back to three or four outward-pointing buds from the base.

• Cut branches of newly planted standard roses.

• On established roses wait until very late fall or spring before pruning.

• If your roses are grown without any underplanting, make sure the area is free of weeds. Loosen soil surface and mulch with organic matter. Remove suckers. Promote ripening with potassium-rich fertilizer.

• Spray roses with funginex every ten days until frost; add dolomite lime to beds at end of October.

• Roses for the Far North (zones 2 and 3): Thérèse Bugnet; Harison's Yellow, John Cabot, Hansa.

ANNUALS AND CONTAINERS

• Start bringing in house plants that have been outside.

• Plant boxes and containers with spring-flowering bulbs (make sure container is more than 35 cm/14 in. in depth and width).

• Hardy annuals to plant now: CALENDULA; CENTAUREA; DELPHINIUM; ESCHSCHOLZIA; IBERIS and NIGELLA.

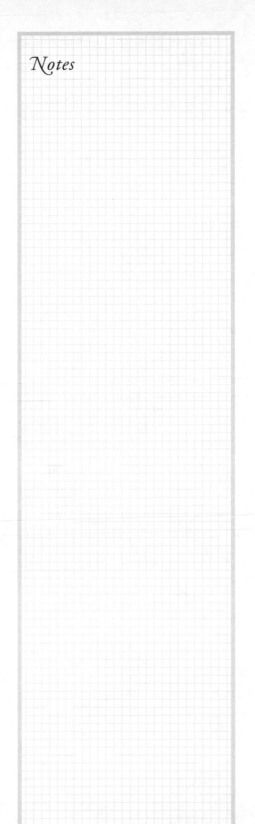

Notes

BULBS

• Start planting bulbs. In some parts of the country freeze-up is looming—so begin mulching.
• Bulbs for shade: ANEMONE NEMOROSA; ENDYMION NON-SCRIPTUS (bluebells, sometimes listed as SCILLA NUTANS); ERANTHIS HYEMALIS (winter aconite) or in flower pots; SCILLA; dog's-tooth violet (ERYTHRONIUM DENS-CANIS). GALANTHUS NIVALIS; G. ELWESII; star-of-Bethlehem (ORNITHOGALUM NUTANS); TULIPA SYLVESTRIS.

Forcing Bulbs I:

When forcing bulbs use large pots and get them in as soon as possible. Jam as many in as you can (almost touching). Make two layers for a spectacular display. The mix should be soil, sand and peat moss in equal parts. Tips of small bulbs should be 20-30 mm/3-4¼ in. below rim of the pot; tips of larger show just above. Put in position. Fill soil to rim, water, label clearly. Store in a cool dark place and don't let dry out. Keep at 4-10°C/40-50°F for twelve to sixteen weeks. Once roots emerge from pot hole, start moving into a warmer space 15°C/60°F—however, no direct light. Then slowly move into brighter light (18 and 22°C/65 and 70°F). Crocuses and daffodils like cooler temperatures; hyacinths and tulips, higher.

Forcing Bulbs II:

Add a bit of charcoal to keep soil sweet; put in bed outdoors, cover with layer of sand; or put in a dark cellar, shed or garage (keep in a black plastic sack); should be 5-7.5 cm/3-5 in. of new growth showing. To develop roots, daffodils take 12-16 weeks, crocus 14 weeks, grape hyacinth 18 weeks, hyacinth 10-11 weeks, iris 10-12 weeks, snowdrops 16 weeks, squill 14 weeks, tulips (single) 7-10 weeks, later cultivars 14-16 weeks.

• Bulbs for outdoor containers: CHIONODOXA (glory-of-the-snow); crocus; CYCLAMEN; C. COUM; C. ALPINUM; ERYTHRONIUM DENS-CANIS (dog's-tooth violet); ERANTHIS (winter aconite); GALANTHUS (snowdrop); IRIS RETICULATA and I. DANFORDIAE; LILIUM CANDIDUM; L. REGALE; L. SPECIOSUM; MUSCARI (grape hyacinth); SCILLA (squill); tulips.

• Bulbs need six months underground but they should be given time enough to develop a strong root system before freeze-up. Prepare soil well and add compost or bulb booster to bottom of planting hole. I like to make a new bulb border with dozens of different kinds from the very tiniest (alliums) to the largest (FRITILLARIA IMPERIALIS); plant them at different depths even with same varieties so they'll come up in succession. Plant three times as deep as widest part of each bulb.

• Tender bulbs such as ACIDANTHERA, cannas, CALADIUM, CROCOSMIA, TIGRIDIA and tuberous begonias must be lifted before frost sets in. When they've turned yellow, remove soil and cut stalk down to 5 cm/2 in.; spread to dry in warm airy sunny place. When dry, lay in flats or open paper bags; store bulblets separately. They like temperatures of about 5°C/40°F and 10°C/50°F. I keep mine in the cellar with the wine and it seems just the right temperature for both.

• Lilies: Dig in lots of compost. Plant European and native lilies, which form roots at base of the bulb, with tips of bulbs not more than 5 cm/2 in. below surface. Stem-rooting lilies (LILIUM REGALE, hybrids) should be set deeper—two to three times the height of bulb. Or at least 15 cm/6 in. deep.

• Stem-rooting lilies should be well covered in pots. Keep adding more soil as shoot grows. Store in a cool place until strong roots form.

• Plant LILIUM CANDIDUM (Madonna lily) higher than others; it's evergreen and will sprout in a few weeks.

• Naturalize bulbs in grass: colchicums, crocus, fritillaria, galanthus, leucojum, narcissus to mimic natural conditions.

Notes

BULB LIST

Source:　　　　　Planted:　　　　　Bloom:　　　　　Ripen:

But don't put them in a place where you'll be mowing before the foliage ripens. Dump bulbs from a basket and plant where they fall. The most graceful bulb display will have species concentrated in drifts and then merging with one another at the edge of the planting.

PERENNIALS

• Stop fertilizing plants in containers; slow down on watering.

• Any shrub roses and hardy container plants to remain outdoors should be fed with potassium-rich fertilizer which will ripen new growth.

• Take cuttings from geraniums, fuchsias and other half-hardy plants. Use nonflowering shoots found near base of the plant, 5-7.5 cm/2-3 in. Remove lower leaves and pot cuttings in mix of damp peat and sand or loam-based soil mix. If you have sandy soil, use your own. Otherwise buy a sterile potting mix. Keep in a cold frame or lightly shaded spot and don't let dry out in warm areas. In colder areas put them in a cool place.

• Take cuttings from plants to overwinter (ones that aren't hardy) like coleus, fuchsia, geraniums, impatiens, marguerites and tender vines. Make a clean cut 12.5 cm/5 in. from tip below a leaf node. Remove bottom few leaves, flowers or buds. Potting mix: ½ peat, ½ perlite; set pot and plant with moistened soil in a plastic bag and close. Keep in a bright window until rooted (two weeks), then repot them separately.

• Divide perennials that seem to be in need of it—they'll start looking dead in the middle. Or will be much too large for the space you've allotted them. This is usually about every three years. Some can go as long as five years untouched. Divide plants only after they've finished flowering. Move to new spots you've prepared by digging down deep; add in compost, manure and water. Replace loam and then settle in plant.

• It's important to keep weeding so seeds won't set and spread.

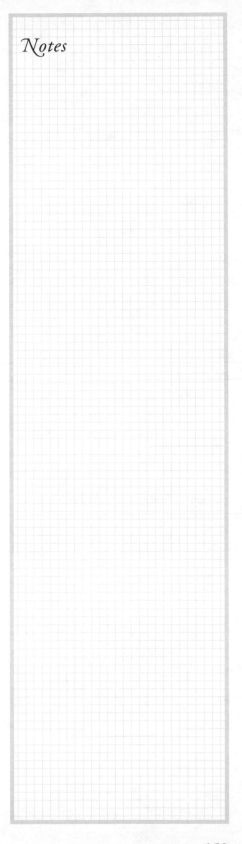

Notes

• These are the plants I have in my garden at this time of year (I live in zone 6):

— ANEMONE X HYBRIDA (Japanese anemone) comes in both pink and white forms. I lean toward A. X HYBRIDA 'Honorine Jobert'.

— Asters are a particular favourite of mine. I'll try any variety. They are the most glorious part of the fall garden: ASTER DUMOSUS; A. NOVAE-ANGLIAE; A. NOVI-BELGII; A. X FRIKARTII 'Monch'; A. X F. 'Wonder von Stava'.

— CARYOPTERIS X CLANDONENSIS (bluebeard or blue mist) flowers on current season's new growth. Previous year's growth should be cut back to two pairs of buds.

— CERATOSTIMGA PLUMBAGINOIDES (leadwort) develops rapidly once it gets going. It is susceptible to severe winterkill but comes back from the roots.

— CIMICIFUGA SIMPLEX; or C. RACEMOSA (snakeroot) makes a gorgeous shower of white, and the most stunning of all, C. R. 'Purpurea', has wonderful purple foliage as well as glorious white flowers.

— NEPETA NERVOSA; N. SIBIRICA (catmint) is twice as tall as the former herbaceous (cut back after first flowering for a second bloom).

— PEROVSKIA ATRIPLICIFOLIA (Russian sage) freezes back to the ground regularly in harsh winters. Treat the same as CARYOPTERIS.

FRUITS, VEGETABLES AND HERBS

• Dig up a few young parsley plants and chives for the cold frame.

• Gather herbs when oils are at their highest.

• Seeds should be collected before they shatter.

• Cut back perennial herbs by two-thirds.

• Pot up chives to be brought indoors.

• Cut out old raspberry canes. Leave one new cane for every 10 cm/4 in. of row. Bend down tops of the canes and tie to supports.

LAWNS

• Repair ragged edges of your lawn this way: cut out a square of turf and reverse it—the ragged edge will send out new growth (or add seeds) into the old lawn.

• Reseed balding patches of lawn if the ground is still warm enough for seeds to germinate. Use a mix of seeds that includes tough local fescues, along with finer seeds. If a disease or bug hits one variety, the lawn will survive with the others. Work up the surface a bit, sow seed and protect with plastic mesh to keep birds from nipping them all out.

• Slow down on mowing the lawn, wait until the grass reaches 7.5 cm/3 in. and slowly raise blades by increments.

• Don't feed lawn any high nitrogen fertilizers from now on. Use a fertilizer high in potash early in the month to encourage root growth.

WATER GARDEN

• Strain out duckweed but leave underwater shoots of oxygenating plants untouched since they'll continue functioning all winter.

• Put protective plastic netting over pools and peg them down around the edges. It allows light in and collects leaves at the same time.

• Pack miniature water gardens in insulating material; install aquarium heater to regulate temperature at 4°C/38°F.

• Tropical water-lilies and other tender aquatics should be brought indoors to a cool spot so they'll stay at near-dormancy.

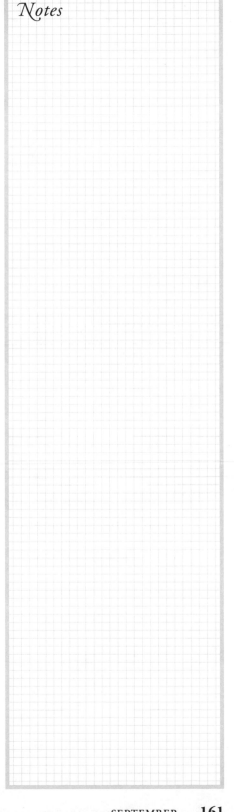

Notes

September

1

2

If you live in the Far North don't plant now, wait until spring;
tender biennials should spend the winter in a cold frame until replanted in spring.

3

Sambucus nigra (elder) will sprout berries; the autumn crocus will emerge.

4

5

6

Planting time for deciduous trees and shrubs begins in late fall after they have naturally shed their leaves. Prepare soil now so it has several weeks to settle in. Dig down at least 45 cm/18 in.; remove all muck and work in lots of compost.

September

Semiripe cuttings root quickly in sandy mixtures or soil.
Keep away from sun the first few weeks.

7

8

9

Prepare new rose beds for planting next month.

Give lots of water to wall-climbing roses.

10

11

You can design your fall garden or a good section of it around roses. It is worthwhile researching the big rose catalogues. Try to use the softer shades since there are enough strident colours everywhere else in the garden. And, as always, make sure they harmonize with what's already there.

12

September

13

Gladiolas: discard old corms and keep the little corms to plant.

14

15

In colder parts of the country, pre-dig places for bulb orders that might arrive after the first frost. This won't hurt the bulbs and will be easier on you.

Always make sure that there's 5-7.5 cm/2-3 in. of good soil below the lily.
Make the hole large enough so the roots can spread out and down.

16

Geraniums (zonal pelargoniums) will thrive if they are pruned back by one-third late in the season, then cut back an equal amount again just before they are moved indoors—to an outward-facing bud so new shoots won't grow inward.

17

18

September

19

Get spots ready for plants that will be delivered later in the fall.
Prepare down to 45-50 cm/18-20 in. Add lots of compost.

20

21

To dry herbs, gather in the morning once the dew has evaporated.
Then rinse, shake and store in sterile containers in a cool dry place.

22

23

Rosemary has to be brought inside for the winter almost everywhere across
the country. Start when you can store it in a house that's relatively cool.

24

September

25

Hardier aquatic plants can remain in place if water doesn't freeze solid.

26

27

Start bringing in house plants that have been summering outdoors while it's still cool indoors. This will lessen the shock of changing the ambience. Make sure you've given all these plants a thorough shower to get rid of pests.

If plants are to be overwintered in the same containers,
get rid of the old soil and repot. Most plants like to be pot-bound.

28

What's in flower now: BOLTONIA ASTEROIDES, *chrysanthemums, coreopsis, gaillardias,*
heleniums, HELIOPSIS HELIANTHOIDES *and rudbeckias. Wild colours seem to be* de rigueur
in the autumn garden. I like to keep them together in the distance and
bring cool colours close to the house.

29

30

October

TREES AND SHRUBS

• Construct wind breaks for azaleas, rhododendrons and any young shrubs by setting up wooden stakes and stapling burlap along the upright stakes.

• Stake new trees by using three stakes leaning in toward the tree at top. Wrap the trunk wherever the stakes touch.

• How to take hardwood cuttings: hardwood feels mature—cut a piece of stem. If you take a piece with heel or a bit of old wood this is called a heel cutting. Trim or cut back just below a pair of leaves or buds. Bury it up from a third to a half of its length directly in garden soil or in the cold frame. In the north take hardwood cuttings in March. You don't need hormone rooting powder. Experiment—it's all free anyway.

• When planting new fruit trees (all of which are grafted) make sure you don't cover the join between the graft and the parent stock.

• Make screens with stakes and wire mesh interwoven with straw or hung with plastic or sacking and use around shrubs, especially evergreens. Remove when temperatures rise and there's no wind.

• For colour in the fall garden try some of these plants: ACER PALMATUM 'Sangokaku' (coral bark maple); A. 'Osakazuki'; A. PALMATUM 'atropurpureum'; A. PALMATUM 'Dissectum'; AMELANCHIER CANADENSIS; COTINUS COGGYGRIA 'Royal Purple' (smoke bush); ENKIANTHUS (pagoda bush); EUONYMUS ALATA (winged euonymus); E. EUROPAEA (European spindle tree); E. SACHALINENSIS (also known as E. PLANIPES); GINKGO BILOBA (maidenhair tree); HYDRANGEA PETIOLARIS (climbing hydrangea); KOELREUTERIA PANICULATA (golden-rain tree); LABURNUM (golden-chain tree); LARIX (larch); LEYCESTERIA FORMOSA (pheasant berry, Himalayan honeysuckle); LIQUIDAMBAR STYRACIFLUA (American sweet-gum, similar to maple tree); MAHONIA AQUIFOLIUM; OXYDENDRUM ARBOREUM (sourwood); PARROTIA PERSICA; RHUS COTINUS.

VINES

• To espalier: attach wires to wall at 40 cm/16 in. intervals from the ground. Train branches along wires. Cut out those that do not conform.

ROSES

• Prepare sites for roses you've ordered. Dig a large hole and mix in lots of compost and manure, add a bit of soil and water deeply. Leave in this condition until you are ready to plant.
• Prune rambler roses.
• Make sure that any vegetation that has been touched by mildew or black spot is picked off the plant. Don't let it sit on the ground or the fungus will overwinter. And don't put any of this in the compost.
• Species shrub roses, climbers and ramblers can be propagated from hardwood cuttings.
• In other parts of the country when the freeze-up is complete, protect plants with a combination of soil and compost. Hill up (about 30 cm/12 in.) with soil and mulch.

ANNUALS

• Pull out any annuals that are looking sad and throw them in the compost.

PERENNIALS

• Don't overtidy the garden. Think of the forest—no one is nipping about with a broom cleaning up. Leave litter on the ground to break down into humus, with the exception of oak and maple leaves which mat when soggy and smother everything underneath. Keep them in another area.

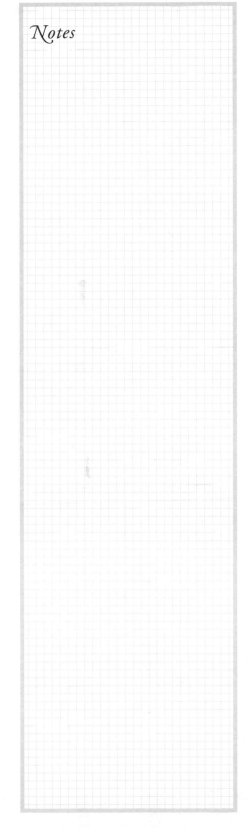

Notes

Try dumping these leaves in a hole and layering them with soil to break down. They will be perfect as leaf mould mulch next year.

• Cut back perennials. Leave enough stalk to protect crowns of plants. They will provide sculptural forms in the winter. Anything with seed heads can be a source of food for birds.

• Don't touch ornamental grasses. They look interesting all winter and can be tidied in the spring.

• What leaves will do for you: they have all the nutrients that plants need including trace minerals; they offer great protection against the freeze-thaw of winter; they break down into organic material over time.

• A deep nest of leaves will succour slugs and mice which will munch away on your favourite plants—one good reason to mulch deeply after the ground is frozen. Most plants, however, will come back from the roots even if they have suffered some winter chomping.

• Add slow-acting fertilizers such as phosphates for next spring's growth. Compost and any other organic matter mixed together will break down slowly and contribute to winter protection.

• Keep on dividing plants if you have several weeks before frost.

• Divide plants about every five years (every three if they get out of hand).

• Plants to protect: dicentra, lunaria, tradescantia.

• I usually label the garden at this time of the year assuming I'll forget everything by next spring.

• Let fallen leaves break down around shrubs (shred maple leaves with the lawn mower).

• Keep planting as long as the ground isn't frozen or too wet.

• In zones 8 and 9 protect agapanthus, camellia, fatsia, lilies and nandina with a cage filled with leaves and protected from the rain.

• Complete bulb planting in northern areas.

- For alpines which don't like rain, use plastic cloches. (Bend wire or canes parallel to each other to form an arc; stretch plastic over top. Bury excess and leave open for good circulation.)
- Put patio containers inside large cardboard cartons and fill with crumpled newspapers; recycle old Styrofoam picnic coolers to store borderline hardy plants.
- Take geraniums (pelargoniums) out of their pots, leave some soil on them and hang in a cool dark place in old panty hose or something that will breathe.
- If last year's poinsettia is still with you, make it bloom again in time for Christmas. Put in a completely dark place for fourteen hours a day and good light for the rest (don't leave in the dark for more than twenty-four hours). Six weeks before Christmas, slowly bring it out to the standard available light.
- When frost blackens the foliage of dahlias, tuberous begonias, gladioli and other summer bulbs, get them ready for storage. Lift, remove soil, wash, remove dead tops, leave a 15 cm/6-in. stem. Divide by using a sharp knife.
- Plants such as fuchsias, geraniums, marguerites and TIBOUCHINA don't have a dormant period. They prefer drought and will do best in a sun room or a cool greenhouse where the temperatures don't dip below 7°C/45°F at night. Prune back when you bring them in. In warm areas, these plants can take a little frost, except for TIBOUCHINA (princess flower). They will survive in a trench or wire cage with 60 cm/2 ft. of dry leaves as mulch, packed loosely to allow air circulation. Cover the top with plastic to keep rain out. Trench method: Prune back by two-thirds, trim root by two-thirds; choose a well-drained protected place so soil won't get waterlogged. Dig the trench 45 cm/18 in.; lay plants on their sides, cover with peat and mark area well. Lift in February or March and repot.
- Sow sweet peas in warm areas.

Notes

FRUITS, VEGETABLES AND HERBS

• If your trees have developed peach leaf curl, pear and apple scab or black knot on plums, you might have to use a fungicide. Use only on dormant trees. In colder climates, treat in spring before buds begin to break—100 g/4 oz. in a litre/quart of water.

• Cut out old or dead wood from apple trees while leaves are still on. Prune out diseased or weak branches and open up to the light as much as possible. Remove crossed wood, cut twiggy growth back to base.

• Place seeds of cherries, apricots, plums, peaches in pots of soil or mix of sand and soil and put in an out-of-the-way spot fully exposed to weather. They'll be ready for sowing in spring.

• Plant winter and spring lettuce now.

• Basil, chives, lemon balm, marjoram, parsley, sage, tarragon and thyme will survive in pots on window sills with enough light. When you lift the plants, take as much root as possible. Water in well and then sparingly thereafter. They will be happiest in a room that's 10-16°C/50-60°F by day 5°C/40°F by night.

LAWNS

• Remove thatch from the lawn with special thatch rake.

• In cold areas fertilize grass as late as possible with a nitrogen fertilizer. This will bump up the production of carbohydrates and will provide early greening up in spring.

• In mild wet areas don't use nitrogen since this will only encourage growth and, perhaps, fungal diseases. Use a fertilizer high in phosphorus and potassium.

• In coastal gardens, make sure you aerate the lawn for good drainage.

• Scythe flower meadow; grasses should never be so tall that they will be lodged (knocked over) by rain and snow—very important if you've got bulbs in there.

NURSERIES

Name:	Address:	Telephone:	Date Visited / $ Spent:

October

1

If frosts come before you and your plants are ready,
throw old sheets over those still blooming just as the light starts to fail.
This will hold the warmth of the day inside through the crucial frigid hours.

2

3

Hold off with serious mulching until after the ground is full of frost.
Make a 10 cm/4 in. layer of dry leaves or straw around vulnerable shrubs.

4

5

6

To keep mice away from trees and shrubs use spiralled plastic or old bleach bottles
(everything should be removed in spring).

October

7

8

9

Mulch fruit trees and shrubs
but don't let mulch touch the stem or rot may set in.

Roses need a lot of water. Give new plants a really good soak, especially if the soil looks dry.

10

Hold off pruning roses until the leaves turn colour and start to fall. The longer you leave them alone, the more time the plant has to store up food and strength against the ravages of winter.

11

12

In warm areas dig around plants to aerate the soil; add compost as mulch.

October

If you live in an area without reliable snow cover, you should mulch your plants.
Be careful not to cover any plant that forms rosettes radiating from the main plant.
Spread organic mulch around base of each plant.

13

14

15

*Dig up herbs such as parsley, chives, mint, oregano
and put in pots for the winter months.*

16

17

18

*Clean up greenhouse or cold frames for the arrival of plants to be overwintered.
Do this on a mild day; wash everything down with a disinfectant.*

October

19

20

Keep rock gardens and beds with small biennials or seedlings cleared of any leaves which might smother small plants.

21

Leave celery and parsnips in the ground so that frost can sweeten them up.

22

*Cut tomatoes with a good length of vine still attached and hang upside down
in a dark place to ripen (put a box beneath to catch the ripened fruit).*

23

24

October

25

Cut foliage of asparagus back to ground once it turns yellow. Mulch with organic matter.

26

27

28

Aerate the lawn by walking over with cramponlike spikes or golf shoes.

29

30

31

It's time for the last mow of the lawn—5 cm/2 in.
Leave clippings in place or use some for a layer on the compost pile.

November

❦

MAINTENANCE

• Ventilate the greenhouse.
• Wash tools off with warm soapy water; remove rust with fine steel wool and dip a rag in vegetable oil to wipe tools clean. This will keep rust away during the winter.

CONTAINERS

• Bring in tender plants once frost threatens. Lots of Mediterranean plants can withstand some frost—let them stay outside as long as possible. What they can't take is freeze-thaw cycles. This is especially true for plants like rosemary.

TREES AND SHRUBS

• In temperate regions, prune as soon as leaves have dropped off apples, pears, plums and other fruit trees—or once the tree is dormant. In pruning the idea is to open up the centre of the tree. Cut leader down by one-third, laterals by two-thirds on a 45° angle above bud, away from the bud. For side shoots, make cuts facing out to avoid growth into the centre.

ROSES

• Remove only dead wood from roses—don't prune until spring.

PERENNIALS

• Plants with grey or hairy, woolly foliage in rock gardens are subject to rot if they get soggy. Make a collar of small pebbles around them.

• Your soil dictates what you can plant in the fall: light sandy soil will have good drainage and is conducive to late planting; heavy soil tends to get wet and might lead to rot—wait for spring to continue planting.

LAWNS

• Get all the weeds out of the lawn now and you'll save yourself an incredible amount of work in the spring. As long as the grass is visible and not frozen solid, you can persist.
• Raise clods of soil in new beds to be broken up; frost will lift the surface. Don't rake it even, this will destroy too much of the life in the soil. Let the weather break it down naturally.
• Get any remaining leaves off the lawn and put in compost. Or put them in bags, slightly moisten. Add soil, bundle up and kick around during the winter to keep them moving. They'll heat up and start to break down.

WATER GARDEN

• Move plants growing in containers to the deepest part of the pond so they won't be subject to freeze.
• Don't worry about water lilies. They die back naturally. Move tropical water lilies to an indoor aquarium or basin.
• Drain pool and cover crowns of water lilies with straw, and the whole pool with plastic.
• Use Styrofoam blocks to absorb expansion of ice in concrete pools.
• In shallow pools, if there is any chance the water will freeze solid, catch fish with a net and bring indoors.
• Air and water pumps, pipes and hoses should be drained, cleaned and brought indoors.

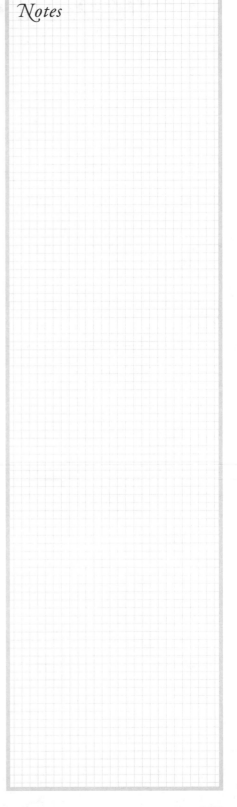

Notes

November

1

2

3

*Clean lawn mowers and all
other equipment ready to store for winter.*

4

Plant large window boxes and containers with small broad-leaved evergreens and conifers, heaths and dwarf winter-flowering shrubs.

5

6

November

7

8

9

Finish raking up leaves, dig new beds.

Get rid of any weeds you see lurking about the garden.

10

In warm areas, finish cleaning up the garden and mulching.
Wet, cold and fog will induce dormancy in plants.

11

12

November

13

14

Trim Michaelmas daisies and delphiniums back about 30 cm/12 in.
This is about the latest to plant tulips. Check bulbs for signs of growth.
If there is 2.5 cm/1 in. or more of leaf and bud, move to a warmer spot.

15

In warm spots heather (ERICA CARNEA) *will be opening.*

16

17

18

November

19

*Cut back withered growth on hardy deciduous plants
or leave dead leaves of tender plants on and clean up next spring.*

20

21

22

23

Moss is a sign of compacted soil—spike (aerate) when ground isn't too wet or hardened by frost.

24

November

Get rid of dead leaves from the pond; clear away untidy foliage after frost has turned it black. Except for reeds and rushes which supply oxygen to the water, cut back all growth.

25

26

27

28

29

30

In very warm areas, mow less frequently,
but never when grass is wet.

December

CHRISTMAS TREES

Christmas trees are bred to be chopped down and die for you. Make sure yours isn't harvested from the wild. There is an alternative good enough to satisfy the greenest of green persons. Consider buying your Christmas tree with the intention of replanting it out of doors.

Buy a small evergreen about 2 m/5 ft. in a 20 L/5 gal. pail. Dig a hole where you want to put the tree later and then fill it with leaves. Save the soil and keep it from freezing. Bring the tree indoors just before Christmas. Don't put it anywhere near a heat or light source. After a maximum of two weeks put it back in the garden. Moisten the hole and plant with warm water. Return soil, and mulch with leaves.

Recycling a Traditional Christmas Tree
• Put some tree branches in window boxes with dried berries and seed pods for added pleasure.
• Use branches for mulch around shrubs and plants.
• Wire branches over trellised vines for protection.
• Use the naked branches as stakes in the spring garden.
• Use the tree for firewood.
• Even if you don't buy a Christmas tree, prowl the lots after the holidays for trees on sale or being thrown out. Do the same in your neighbourhood. These are incredibly valuable to your garden.

Buying a Christmas Tree
• When buying a Christmas tree make sure it hasn't been dipped in dye to appear fresh. Press the needles back to make sure of freshness. Then run your hand across the bottom—if it's sticky it's fresh. Always put it in a large container of water and keep the water topped up daily.

Look Around the Garden for Christmas Bouquets
• Artemisias can be the basis for wreaths (smells good too).
• GALIUM VERUM (yellow or Our-Lady's-bedstraw) can be used in a basket of dried flowers or a manger.
• MYRTUS COMMUNIS (myrtle) can be used in wreaths and garlands.

Christmas Gifts for Gardeners
• A pair of goatskin gloves will leave hands feeling lovely after working in the garden.
• A box of bag balm—really—this lanolin rich salve is used for the sore nipples on cows. It works wonders for gardener's hands (chapped, rough) and feet (sore).
• A long-spouted watering can. These are great for getting into neglected spots at the back of the border.
• A self-standing bag. Various brand names for this useful item—it stands alone wherever you slam it down. Great for weeding, leaf-raking and just gathering things up from the garden.

TREES AND SHRUBS
• Make sure that roses are well mulched to avoid freeze-thaw fluctuations. Put climbers and ramblers on ground and cover with soil and branches from evergreens.

Shrubs for Winter Interest
• Here are some shrubs that will provide winter interest whether it's from evergreen foliage or colourful twigs:

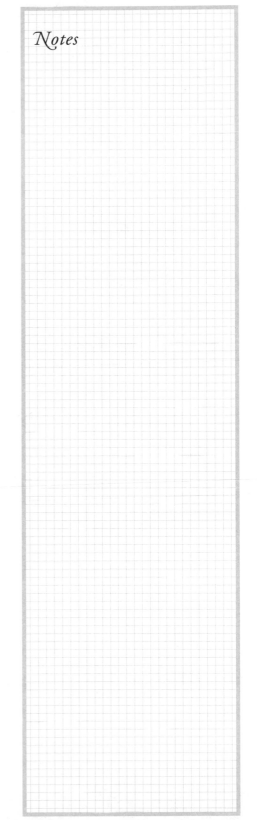

Notes

• MAHONIA AQUIFOLIUM (Oregon holly-grape, Z5), prune to keep it in scale and not to flop over. It turns burgundy in winter, comes back from the stem in spring with bright green almost yellow shiny leaves, then has brilliant green leaves until fall when it turns scarlet.

• COTONEASTER DAMMERI; C. HORIZONTALIS—these cotoneasters have wonderful green leaves and bright red berries.

• PYRACANTHANA (firethorn) has gorgeous coloured berries in the winter.

• VIBURNUM DAVIDII retains its green leathery leaves.

• ACER PALMATUM (Japanese maple)—the shapes are so beautiful against the snow that they are hard to ignore.

• ERICA CARNEA 'Springwood White'; E. C. 'Vivellii' (red) are winter heathers.

• HEDERA HELIX (English Ivy) is evergreen and it will grow from zone 6 up as will pachysandra and vinca.

• HAMAMELIS (witch hazel, yellow). You will enjoy this shrub for its scent as well.

• Shrubs with brightly coloured twigs. CORNUS ALBA 'Sibirica' (red osier dogwood); C. STOLONIFERA 'flaviramea' (yellow dogwood). KERRIA JAPONICA (Z4) has green twigs all winter. Prune back early in spring for the best stems in winter.

• EUONYMUS EUROPAEA (European spindle tree) has berries in fall in pink clusters, orange seeds inside. ELAEAGNUS UMBELLATA (autumn olive) has silver foliage, drops in fall and shows off its silver bark; CORYLUS AVELLANA 'contorta' (Harry Lauder's walking stick) looks very dramatic in my garden with lights behind its weird shape.

• EUONYMUS MAS has winter flowers in zones 7 and warmer.

• PRUNUS SUBHIRTELLA 'autumnalis' (flowering cherry) has good colour; STEWARTIA PSEUDOCAMELLIA (false camellia); CALLICARPA (beautyberry) has the most amazing coloured berries if you have both male and female; PERNETTYA MUCRONATA (huckleberry) is a native; PARTHENOCISSUS

QUINQUEFOLIA (Virginia creeper) is gorgeous in fall in any zone.

• Shrubs for warmer areas: ACER DAVIDII (Père David's maple); winter jasmine has golden yellow flowers in autumn; winter-flowering plum has leaves which drop in November and blossoms all winter. Figs, kiwi, loquats will need a bit of protection with a chicken wire cage 30 cm/12 in. high.

• Watch for treacherous freeze-thaw cycles from now on. If there has been a thaw and the weather is dry and sunny, it's best to water evergreens. This seems strange but they transpire or give off water all the time and are prone to drying out—drastically. There are effective antidesiccants but get them in spray bottles not cans—easier on the environment.

THE SOIL

To lower pH (make more acid): dig in well-soaked sphagnum peat moss, or add sulphur 135 g per sq m (5¾ oz. per sq yd.).

To raise pH (make more alkaline):
sandy soil – add lime 270 g per sq m (11½ oz. per sq yd.);
loam – add lime 540 g per sq m (22½ oz. per sq yd.);
heavy clay – add lime 800 g per sq m (35 oz. per sq yd.).

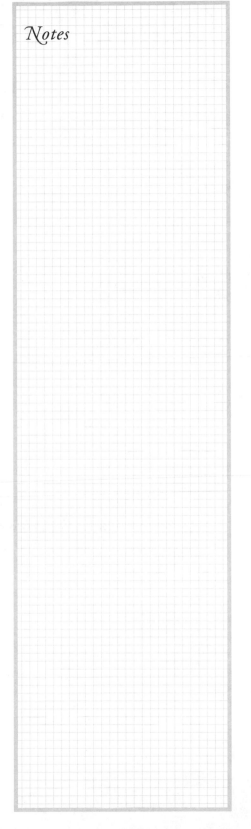

Notes

December

1

2

Prune summer-flowering shrubs by cutting out the oldest wood and anything dead (you should mark this before the leaves fall). Do this as early in the month as possible.

3

*After Christmas, tie the tree or just the branches to a fence
and tie popcorn, fruit or suet on it for birds to eat.*

4

*Use an old or abandoned Christmas wreath
as mulch around acid-loving plants such as azaleas.*

5

6

December

7

Use the tips of evergreen branches for sachets or potpourris.

8

9

10

Chop up the tree and collect all needles as mulch for acid-loving plants.

11

12

*Rosemary is pleasant used in
wreaths, pomanders, teas, jellies and in cooking.*

13

December

14

15

16

Homemade potpourri: 454 ml/1 pint of pine needles, 227 ml/1 cup citrus peel, 227 ml/1 cup each of basil, bay, rosemary and 454 ml/2 cups coarse salt.

Plants for Christmas: of course,
the traditional Christmas cactus, poinsettia, kalanchoe.

17

Watch evergreens in containers on balconies and terraces. Give them a large drink
of cool water (not warm) if there are very many dry days in a row.

18

19

December

20

Pruning of grapes is done during Capricorn's rule (December 22 to January 19) when the moon is in the second quarter. Grapes, we are told, will grow round and juicy with the swelling moon.

21

22

Free branches of snow as soon as possible after a heavy wet snowfall.
Shake them but don't pull them or they'll snap.

23

24

25

Other evergreen plants: HELLEBORUS NIGER *(Christmas rose);*
the graceful lines of BETULA PENDULA *(weeping birch)*
is a winter treat almost everywhere in the country.

December

26

27

28

Use lavender in sachets and bouquets.

If your ground isn't frozen solid this is a good time to amend it.

29

The four-season garden is a marvellous thing.
Winter snows should not inhibit your garden enjoyment and
it's a good time to evaluate the bones or understructure of your garden.

30

31

SELECTED BIBLIOGRAPHY

Cambell, Stuart. *Let It Rot!: The Gardener's Guide to Composting*. Pownal, Vermont: Garden Way Publishing, 1975

Evans, Hazel. *Gardening Through the Year*. Great Britain: Orbis Book Publishing Corp. Ltd., 1985

Ferguson, John and Burkhardt Mucke. *The Gardener's Year*. Toronto: Barron's, 1991

Firth, Grace. *A Natural Year*. New York: Simon and Schuster, 1972

Franck, Gertrud. *Companion Planting*. Wellingborough, England: Thorsons Publishing Group, 1983

Galston, Arthus W. *Green Wisdom*. New York: Perigee, 1981

Harris, Marjorie. *The Canadian Gardener*. Toronto, Random House of Canada, 1990

Harris, Marjorie. *Ecological Gardening*. Toronto: Random House of Canada, 1991

Lee, Albert. *Weather Wisdom*. Chicago: Congdon & Weed, 1976

Riotte, Louise. *Astrological Gardening*. Pownal, Vermont: Garden Way Publishing, 1989

Smith, Miranda and Anna Carr. *Rodale's Garden Insect, Disease & Weed Identification Guide*. Emmaus, Pa: Rodale Press, 1988

Stout, Ruth. *How to Have a Green Thumb Without an Aching Back*. New York: Fireside Books, 1987

Tarrant, David. *A Year In Your Garden*. Vancouver: Whitecap Books, 1989

Tarrant, David. *Pacific Gardening Guide*. Vancouver: Whitecap Books, 1990

Encyclopaedias:

Encyclopedia of Organic Gardening, The. Emmaus, Pa.: Rodale Press, 1978

Encyclopedia of Natural Insect & Disease Control. Emmaus, Pa.: Rodale Press, 1984

Hortus Third. New York: Macmillan, 1976

Wyman, Donald. *Wyman's Gardening Encyclopedia,* 2nd ed. New York: Macmillan, 1986

Magazines:

Canadian Gardening. 131 Spy Court, Markham, Ont., L3R 5H6

Gardens West. 1090 W. 8th Ave., Box 1680, Vancouver, B.C., V6B 3W8

Island Grower. The, R.R. 4, Sooke, B.C., V0X 1N0

Organic Gardening. 33 East Minor St., Emmaus, Pa, 180098 U.S.A.

Prairie Garden, The. P.O. Box 517, Winnipeg, Man., R3C 2J3

COGnition. 25 Sandbar Willoway, Willowdale, Ont., M2J 2B1

INDEX

M

N

O

P